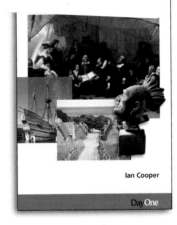

Ian Cooper

DayOne

Series Editor: Brian H Edwards

DayOne

The **Pilgrim Fathers:** The promise and price of religious freedom

⑥ The storm breaks

The original vision of reaching the Natives with the gospel had been largely lost in the struggle to survive. Foremost of the few who had a heart for the Natives was John Eliot — the 'Apostle to the Indians'

The Place of Hills

Having worked with Thomas Hooker at Little Baddow, John Eliot migrated to America in 1631 where he initially accepted a call to the ministry of the 1ivy congregation in Roxbury. The town was one of the first six settlements planted by the Massachusetts Bay Colony in 1630, with its inhabitants forming the congregation of the First Church. Eliot became concerned for the salvation of the Natives and, with the help of a young Native began learning the language. He preached at Newtown in 1646 where a member of the Natives confessed faith in Jesus Christ, including one named Wabam who was the first convert to Christianity from his tribe. Others soon followed. Eliot made representations to the Massachusetts General Court for the setting aside of land for these converted Natives along with provision for the preaching of the gospel to them. Supporters in England were keen to make

funds available when they heard of Eliot's work and the 'Society for the Propagation of the Gospel in New England' was formed in 1649. Eliot established a town at Natick, now in the western suburbs of Boston, for the 'Praying Indians' as they became known. In time several other such towns were formed although Natick is the only one which retain ats original Indian name. Others joined the effort to reach the Natives with the gospel and by 1674 it was believed that there were 4000 converted Native People.

John Eliot's most important work, however, was his translation of the Scriptures into the Native language. He began with a translation of the Ten Commandments and The Lord's Prayer, but by 1663 the whole Bible was in the Algonquian tongue — the very first Bible to be printed in America. Along with the gift of the word of God in their own language, Eliot also gave them the gift of literacy and education. He was aided in his translation work by a

Facing page: The site of the meeting house at Natick

Top: Natick Historical Society Museum. Eliot's Native (Algonquian) language Bible is here

Middle: Burial site of Daniel Takawampbait, a converted Native who became Natick's minister

Below: Memorial to John Eliot in Natick park

Above: Map showing Natick's memorials to the work of John Eliot

converted Native by the name of Wassammon who took the Christian name of John Sassamon and who served as schoolmaster at Natick. Eliot took Sassamon to Harvard College for a time in 1653 where he engaged in study even before Harvard started its 'Indian Harvard' two years later. Sassamon eventually became minister of the church at Namasket in 1673. Tragically, it would be his suspicious death in 1675 that precipitated the horrors of the conflict known as 'King Philip's War'.

'King' Philip

In July 1662, Massasoit's eldest son and leader of the Pokanokets, Alexander, was fishing on

Monponsett Pond, Halifax, Massachusetts, when he was surprised by Josiah Winslow and ten well armed men. Winslow had been commissioned to bring Alexander to court on account of his unauthorised selling of land to Rhode Islanders who were not bound by the rules of the United Colonies of New England. Such trade jeopardised the stability and supremacy of the Plymouth colony and needed to be brought to a halt. As Alexander reluctantly made his way to a meeting of the magistrates at Duxbury, he fell ill and was taken to Mount Hope where he died. Suspicion and rumour increased the tensions between the Plymouth colony and the Natives

who were already feeling that the English no longer valued or cared for them. Thousands of Natives gathered at Mount Hope to mourn the loss of Alexander and also to acknowledge the appointment of the twenty four year old Philip, Massasoit's other son, as Sachem of the Pokanokets. The magistrates at Plymouth were so concerned as to what this great gathering might mean that they called Philip to appear before them, fearing he was preparing for war. Philip's demeanour there earned him the nickname 'King Philip'; however he did reaffirm the covenant that had existed between his father and the settlers and it seemed that relations

CONTENTS

© Day One Publications 2015 First printed 2015

A CIP record is held at The British Library   ISBN 978 1 84625 477 5

Published by Day One Publications Ryelands Road, Leominster, HR6 8NZ

🕾 01568 613 740 FAX 01568 611 473 email: sales@dayone.co.uk www.dayone.co.uk   All rights reserved

Design: Steve Devane design.com Printed by PB Print

Dedication: In memory of Harry Curwood

The Pilgrim Fathers

Even today the name 'Mayflower' is recognised by most people – it brings to mind a romantic tale of godly men and women in search of a new start on the far side of the ocean. Few, however, know of the conditions which set these folk on their perilous journey, nor the years of exile in Europe long before the Mayflower set sail. Neither do they know that even before arriving in the hostile environment of the New World, the 'Pilgrims' had been deceived, betrayed and intermingled with others whose goal was not Christian purity but financial gain.

On 13 November 1620, in a scene faintly reminiscent of Noah's first steps from the ark onto dry ground, the passengers of the Mayflower stepped from their ship after sixty–five days at sea. Like Noah, they would soon realise that the corruptions they sought so hard to escape had followed hard on their heels. The faithful, Puritan settlers were godly, courageous, and earnest in their desire to worship the God of heaven in simplicity and truth, but they were not without fault and their new environment was hostile, and many of their fellow travellers had little enthusiasm for their spiritual ideals. Within a few months of arriving, half of them would be dead. What awaited the remainder were years of hardship, conflict and disappointment before the struggling Plymouth colony saw its significance fade in the wake of other expeditions settling to the north in Boston. However, the impact these men and women made on the world continues today, not least in the 'New England' which they settled, populated and evangelised over many generations.

There is often confusion as to what we should call the people that the Pilgrims came into contact with on their arrival in New England. This guide uses the accepted term Natives or Native People to refer to the inhabitants of the land when the settlers arrived. Where quotes from the settlers are used, their terms have not been changed; likewise, where the Natives were referred to as 'Praying Indians', that description has been retained.

Facing page: Mayflower II — Plymouth Harbour (MA)

1 Setting sail

The little village of Scrooby in Nottinghamshire seems an unlikely place for a revolution, but it was here, in the beginning of the 17th century, that the seeds of spiritual discontent were sown to the extent that a small group of 'Pilgrims' began their journey to New England

They were not the first to make the journey and their route was a rather tortuous one, but their story is the stuff of legend. Others had ventured to the shores of North America, but these attempts had often been attended by disaster. As early as 1584 Sir Walter Raleigh obtained a charter to establish a colony in what is now known as North Carolina. Raleigh himself never went there, but his agent, Sir Richard Grenville, arrived at Roanoke Island in 1585 with 107 settlers. However, these all chose to return to England when Sir Francis Drake visited the island the following year. Raleigh sponsored another expedition of 150 colonists in 1587, but a supply ship sent three years later found the settlement deserted and dismantled. There have been many theories as to the disappearance of the Roanoke colonists but it remains a mystery to this day. In St. Brides Church in Fleet Street, London, there is a memorial to the young Virginia Dare who was born in the Roanoke Colony in 1587. Her grandfather was John White, the Governor, who returned to

Above: Scrooby Church was the Parish Church of William Brewster's family until he disagreed with Anglican ritual and unlawfully absented himself from worship to join a Separatist meeting

Facing page: The village in Nottinghamshire as it is today. Scrooby became the epicentre of religious dissent in the early 17th century

England at the end of 1587 to collect supplies. When he was finally able to return in 1590 everyone had disappeared and there was no trace of his family or granddaughter.

In 1607 another expedition had settled at Jamestown in Virginia but this was established largely for the purposes of trade. Under the charter of the Virginia Company, the settlers experienced turbulent times arising mainly through their harsh treatment of the Natives and their lack of preparedness for the conditions they found. A shortage of food, bitter water and disease almost destroyed the colony which was only saved by a fresh batch of English colonists arriving with supplies just in time in 1610.

The fledgling Church of England, under the reign of Elizabeth I, was a place of great

Above: *The memorial to Virginia Dare in St Brides Church, London – the first child born in the ill-fated Roanoke colony*

tension. Whilst the Queen had broken with Rome, she preferred many of its practices and rituals to the simpler worship of the Reformers, many of whom she disliked and regarded as dangerous fanatics. Elizabeth began a process of reformation and reconciliation resulting in the 1563 'Elizabethan Religious Settlement' which sought to promote Protestantism without completely alienating the mass of the population which had turned to Roman Catholicism during the reign of Mary.

Many had fled to the Continent to escape Mary's bloody reign of persecution in which around 300 men, women and children were executed for their Protestant faith (see in this series *The Martyrs of Mary Tudor* by Andrew Atherstone). At last they could return to their homeland and pursue their goal of returning simplicity of worship to the Church of the Lord Jesus Christ. Their efforts were constantly thwarted, however, by Elizabeth's own hesitation. The 'Settlement' was a compromise which many could not live with and which actually preserved many of the rites and forms which they detested. Elizabeth insisted on adherence to the Thirty Nine Articles and forbade unlicensed preaching or printing of religious material. The Bishops of the Court of High Commission ruthlessly enforced the Queen's dictates and many faithful men were consigned to prisons without representation or hope of defence.

Those who longed to see the end of clerical vestments, the 'sign

Above: *Replica ships* Susan Constant, Discovery *and* Godspeed *at Historic Jamestown, Virginia*

of the cross', dispensations and countless other relics from the Roman Church, sought instead a simpler form of worship, regaining the ancient purity of the church. In 1565 Archbishop Parker called them 'these Precise men', giving rise to the name 'Precisians' which soon gave way to the more familiar 'Puritans'. Those who ignored or disobeyed the church hierarchy were called 'Non–Conformists' and they were divided into two camps: whilst many genuine believers preferred to stay in the Church of England and attempt to refine it from within, for others it was becoming intolerable; the Church was contaminated and there was only one course of action open to those who saw no real hope for it – separation. Often the distinction is made between Puritans and Separatists, but the division is not as straighforward as that.

The Puritan Ideal

To the modern mind, Puritanism was an aberration – a cult of joyless moralisers who preached a 'dry as dust' gospel of self–denial. This is a sad misrepresentation of the faithful, godly men and women who strove to regain a sense of the glory of Christ in his church. The purity they longed for was first of all doctrinal, then practical – flowing out of hearts moved by the truth of God's word and driven by his Spirit. Dr D M Lloyd–Jones described 'essential Puritanism' as 'a life of spiritual, personal religion, an intense realization of the presence of God, a devotion of the entire being to him.' J I Packer commented 'Seeing life whole, they integrated contemplation with action, worship with work, labour with rest, love of God with love of neighbour and of self.'

Though they are often remembered most for what they objected to – vestments, signs, rites and ornament for example – they were not in themselves negative people. The Puritans loved the Lord's Day. They rejoiced in the gift that God had given them in the Sabbath and made the most of the day's spiritual benefits and blessings. Substantial sermons were preached – often an hour or more in length – and these were applied to the daily lives of the hearers. Psalms and paraphrases of Scriptures were sung in joyful worship and times of prayer were sincere and refreshing. The first book printed in America was the Bay Psalm (hymn) Book of 1640. They loved the Bible and were not content with superficial reading of the Scriptures. This was the breathed-out Word of God to them and they held it in high honour. They believed that the Scriptures had application to all of life, which, in turn was an act of worship in and of itself. Personal Bible reading and self examination were part of the routine of daily life.

Doctrinally the Puritans were essentially Calvinistic, holding to the doctrines of predestination and election. Work and rest alike were means of bringing God glory. Each person was encouraged to use their gifts and talents in serving God, no matter what their vocation. Idleness was considered an especially grievous sin, comparable to drunkenness. The family was regarded as a microcosm of the church itself. Established by God at the pinnacle of his creation, it was considered the foundation stone of all of life, and marriage was regarded as a sacred bond of love between husband and wife. Children were prized and prayed for, educated in the knowledge of the Scriptures and shared in the regular times of family worship which marked the Puritan day. Children of Christian parents were 'baptized' a few days after birth, but only those whose lives demonstrated the transforming effects of the gospel were admitted to membership of the church.

They also valued community highly. The meetinghouse was the centre of community life where both religious and social order was maintained. In the New World, godly men were tasked with establishing biblically based rules for God's glory and the community's well–being.

New King – new hopes

The 1593 Act Against Puritans made it illegal to hold independent meetings outside of the established church and stated that people who did not attend the services of the Church of England for forty days, and who attended private services 'contrary to the laws and statutes of the realm and being thereof lawfully convicted shall be committed to prison, there to remain without bail… until they shall conform and yield themselves to same church.'

James I of England came to the throne in 1603 and there were high hopes for reform of the Church of

Above: The accession of James I of England raised hopes of the reformation of the Church of England, but he disappointed the Puritans and treated them with contempt. (Painting by John de Critz the Elder. Original in Dulwich Picture Gallery)

Below: Detail from the exterior of St Wilfred's (Scrooby) Church, Nottinghamshire. Once the seat of the Archbishops of York – in whose palace Separatist meetings were held

England. Sadly these were dashed when James reinforced rules which endorsed the authority of the church hierarchy and enforced rituals which many Christians found abhorrent.

The Hampton Court Conference of 1604 was a turning point when James I treated a delegation of dissenting men with contempt, making them wait in an antechamber for four days and then summarily dismissing their contributions and pleas. Incredibly, it was at this conference that the king agreed to the suggestion of John Reynolds that a new translation of the Scriptures be undertaken, resulting in the King James Bible being produced. Other than this extraordinary outcome, the case for reforming the Anglican Church seemed hopeless, indeed, the king seemed to be hardened in his attitude towards the Separatists and Puritans alike, threatening to 'harry them out of the land'.

Early Non-conformists

Of the Nottinghamshire Non–conformists, one of the most notable was **William Brewster** who lived in Scrooby Manor where his father, William Brewster Senior, was Bailiff–Receiver. He had been appointed by the Archbishop of York in 1575. His position involved collecting rents from farms and villages around. The younger William lived in these grand surroundings for five years before attending Cambridge University, during which time he came under the influence of others who agitated for genuine spiritual reform in the church.

After completing his studies, Brewster made his way to London where he entered the service of Sir William Davison, one of Queen Elizabeth's Ministers of State. However, in 1587, Davison was committed to the Tower of London as a scapegoat for Elizabeth when the document ordering Mary Queen of Scots' execution – which had been in Davison's possession – was released and the order carried out. Brewster stayed with his master during the two years of his incarceration but returned to Scrooby Manor in 1589 where he took up the position of Postmaster. It was during this time that he aligned himself with the Separatist congregation there. He married Mary in 1591/2 and became the father of Jonathan in 1593. Brewster was ordered to attend York to appear before the Court of High Commission and was fined £20 for being 'disobedient in matters of religion'. He had succeeded his father as Bailiff–Receiver but resigned his post in September 1607. Against the backdrop of oppression and intimidation, a daughter born to Brewster at this time was rather ominously named Fear!

Robert 'Troublechurch' Browne had so stirred up passions in Cambridge by his Puritan style of ministry that he had been forced to 'retire' to Norwich where he was imprisoned by the bishop for holding 'private meetings'. He was later released, but in 1581 decided to head for the Netherlands where he planted a church at Middleburg. Although his desire was to establish a congregation based purely on New Testament principles, the fellowship quickly broke down and was dissolved within two years.

Around this time **John Smyth** came to Gainsborough in Lincolnshire. He was a Non–

Below: Gainsborough Old Hall where John Smyth held Non–conformist meetings

Left: All Saints Church, Babworth, where Richard Clyfton preached from 1586 until 1604 when he was forced to leave due to his Separatist inclinations

Below, left: The Manor House, Austerfield. The birthplace of William Bradford

conformist and a follower of 'Troublechurch' Browne. An Anglican minister, Smyth came to reject the liturgy of the church as the invention of sinful men and was so insistent on the Spirit-led or spontaneous nature of worship that he even forbade the reading of the Bible in meetings as he regarded the translation of the Scriptures also as the product of sinful minds! He was dismissed in 1602 by his employer, the Bishop of Lincoln, for preaching 'strange doctrines'.

Various dissenting believers began to attend Gainsborough on the Lord's Day. However, Smyth's religious views were constantly shifting and his growing congregation was split into two and the smaller of the two groups began to meet at Scrooby, often in the Manor House itself. **Richard Clyfton**, former Rector of Babworth Church had been forced by the church hierarchy to resign his Church of England post in 1604 and became pastor of this little flock.

In the turmoil of those days it was suggested that the congregation should emigrate to Holland and follow Smyth who had already settled there.

John Robinson also joined the fellowship at Scrooby, having been won to the Puritan cause at Cambridge. He had been Associate Pastor at St.

Andrews church in Norwich but was forced to leave by the king's insistence that ministers follow the liturgy. Robinson soon became the assistant to Richard Clyfton. The meetings were, of course, unlawful and unpopular with locals who harassed the congregation, and in 1607 the authorities arrested some of its members.

William Bradford was born in Austerfield, Yorkshire in 1589/90. He had a traumatic childhood, with all his closest relatives having died by the time he was just seven years of age, forcing him to be cared for by uncles who owned a farm. William showed neither aptitude, nor

health for farm work and spent much of his time reading the Scriptures. At the age of twelve he heard Richard Clyfton preach at Babworth and was inspired by what he heard. He continued to attend the services conducted by Clyfton and met William Brewster who befriended him. At the age of eighteen, Bradford travelled to Holland and later to New England with Brewster and became a rich source of information on the new colony through his journal and writings – in particular *Of Plimoth Plantation* in which Bradford recorded his recollections and impressions of the first thirty years of the colony, giving insight into the ideals

Left: Austerfield Church where William Bradford was baptized

Below, left: The 'Bradford Font' at Austerfield Church

Right: Boston Guildhall where it is believed many of the Pilgrims were detained after their failed attempt to flee the country

and struggles of the fledgling community. Bradford later became the Governor of Plymouth and held the post for around thirty years.

Betrayed

It was no easy decision, but after much heart searching the majority of the congregation at Scrooby decided to leave for Holland, a place where religious freedom was reportedly upheld and they would be able to practice their 'true' worship unimpeded. Those who could, sold land and possessions, hoping not to arouse the suspicions of the authorities, and arrangements were made to meet with a ship on the Wash near Boston in Lincolnshire towards the end of 1607. After a disconcerting delay of several days the ship appeared and the party boarded at Scotia Creek and paid their fare, only to discover that the ship's master had

betrayed them to the authorities. The passengers were arrested, roughly treated – even the women to the point of indecency – and imprisoned in Boston for several weeks before being released. Even though many of them now had no homes to go to, they returned to Scrooby where a second attempt to slip away from England was arranged with a Dutch captain.

In the spring of 1608 the party made their way to a remote common between Hull and Grimsby towards an awaiting ship. Bad weather delayed the boarding and the families were taken in by locals for the night – which unfortunately came to the notice of the authorities. The next day, as the women and children attempted to board, the wind drove their boat onto a mud bank at Killingholme Creek where they became trapped. Half of the men were transported to the ship by a boat which turned to collect the remainder. At this

Below: Pilgrim memorial at Scotia Creek commemorates the first attempt by the Scrooby Seperatists to leave England for the Netherlands – and their betrayal by the master of the ship they hired for the purpose

Bottom: Memorial to the Pilgrims at Killingholme Creek marking the second, frustrated, attempt to leave England

time the skipper noticed a crowd on the common apparently intent on detaining the Scrooby rebels. He weighed anchor, hoisted sails and the ship was driven out into the North Sea. Those remaining on land were forced to flee the mob, but many decided to wade out to rescue the women and children from the stranded boat. Although they were then seized they were soon released to return, once again, to Scrooby. Those on board ship suffered a tempestuous two-week journey to Amsterdam.

As a consequence of this turbulent beginning, the number of people now willing to travel to Holland was considerably reduced. However, some were determined to make the break from 'old' England. Instead of a mass escape, family by family and one by one they made their way across the channel where they gathered in Amsterdam to begin what they hoped would be a new and unfettered life of worship and devotion to Christ. Daily life was hard for they found themselves in a strange land, unable to understand the language and in desperate need of finance. They took whatever low–paid employment they could and scraped a meagre living, glad simply to be free of the corruptions of the established church in 17th Century England.

The Ancient Brethren
In Amsterdam there was already a church of dissenting English 'refugees' named the 'Brethren of the Separation of the First English Church at Amsterdam', better known as

Bishop William Laud

William Laud, short in stature but high in ambition, rose to prominence when Charles 1 came to the throne in 1625. He was a passionate opponent of reform of the church, which he believed had already gone too far; he insisted that wooden tables used for the sacraments were replaced with stone altars. Laud vehemently opposed the Puritans who complained that he was sending the church back in the direction of Rome, and used his influence with the king to resist their efforts. Charles made him Bishop of London in 1628 and Archbishop of Canterbury in 1633, in which time he ruthlessly pursued those who defied the king's command concerning church order and ritual. In 1637, Puritans John Bastwick, Henry Burton and William Prynne were arrested on the orders of Laud and had their ears cut off, their noses slit, and were branded on their cheeks SL (Seditious Libeller), for writing pamphlets that criticized the Bishop. Laud precipitated a crisis when he insisted that the churches in Scotland adhere to the English Prayer Book. The Scots defied the order and sent an army into northern England in what became known as the Bishops' Wars. Charles needed to raise his own army to defend the cause but could not, forcing him to call on Parliament for aid. Parliament used the king's need to its own advantage: the price of their support was impeachment for Laud who was detained in the Tower of London. Although the trial ended after twenty days without a vote, he was ultimately beheaded on Tower Hill on 10 January 1645.

Pictured: *Bishop William Laud. Portrait by Sir Anthony van Dyck currently in the National Portrait Gallery, London*

the 'Ancient Brethren'. There were already over three hundred communicants. This church had been settled since the 1590s, led by Francis Johnson and Henry Ainsworth. William Bradford wrote of Ainsworth that he was 'A man of a thousand... very modest, amiable, and of an innocent and unblamable life and conversation, of a meek spirit, and a calm temper, void of passion, and not easily provoked....He had an excellent gift of teaching and opening the Scriptures; and things did flow from him with that facility, plainness and sweetness, as did much affect the hearers.... he was most ready and pregnant in the Scriptures, as if the book of God had been written in his heart..." John Smyth also had about eighty of his Gainsborough congregation with him and Clyfton had a much smaller group from Scrooby.

Sadly, the Ancient Brethren were plagued with divisions and there were persistent rumours about scandalous conduct within the congregation. Once again, the Scrooby refugees found themselves in an intolerable position, this time being associated with a church renowned in the locality for squabbles and immorality. The need to move on became pressing and in 1609 John Robinson went to Leiden (Leyden) where the town authorities agreed to accept them – much to the annoyance of King James I who sent his ambassador to protest against the conduct of the Leiden authorities.

On 1 May 1609 the Gainsborough and Scrooby

'Pilgrims' moved on to Leiden – but without Richard Clyfton who stayed with the Ancient Brethren. It appears that Smyth had openly rejected his own baptism as an infant and rebaptized several of his congregation – including himself. Division occurred over the Biblical warrant for infant baptism with Smyth calling those who supported it 'heretics'. This led to schism within the fellowship and no doubt prompted Robinson, who had begun to soften his attitude towards differing practices of true believers, to seek a new place to worship. Conversely, a number of the Ancient Brethren, tired of the disputes in their own fellowship, decided to go with John Robinson to Leiden. After two years this united congregation acquired a property on Kloksteeg near St Peters Church which became known as the Gronepoort (or the Green Gate).

Facing page: The East Gate — the Zijlpoort at Leiden dates from the 17th century. John Robinson pastored the Puritan refugees in Leiden for around 12 years

Above: Leiden University Buildings. Jacobus Arminius (whose teachings gave rise to the Arminian controversy) studied here from 1576 to 1582

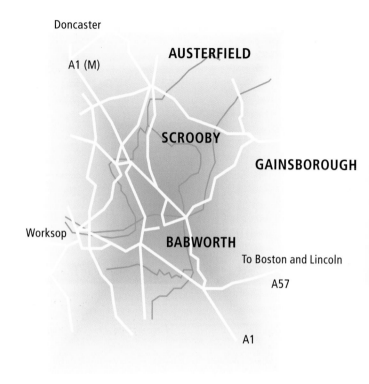

Doncaster

AUSTERFIELD

A1 (M)

SCROOBY

GAINSBOROUGH

Worksop

BABWORTH

To Boston and Lincoln

A57

A1

Above: Map showing Pilgrim sites in and around Nottinghamshire

TRAVEL INFORMATION

Lincolnshire and Nottinghamshire

For downloadable maps of historic sights associated with the Pilgrim Fathers, including self guided and conducted tours – www.pilgrimfathersorigins.org Further tours can be found at www.pilgrimsandprophets.co.uk
Gainsborough Old Hall
Parnell Street, Gainsborough, DN21 2NB
   Built in 1460 this extensive manor is now owned by English Heritage and is open to the public as a museum. In the late 1500's the house was owned by the Hickman family who were sympathetic to the Separatist cause and allowed Smyth, Robinson, Brewster and Bradford to hold meetings in the premises.
   Website: gainsboroughholdhall.com

All Saints' Church, Babworth

Bridle Path, Babworth, Nottinghamshire, DN22 7BP
   The present building dates from the 15th century and the church became a centre for the Separatist cause when Richard Clyfton preached here. The church still holds items from the period, including the cup Clyfton used for communion services.

St Helena's Church

High St, Austerfield, Doncaster DN10 6QU

William Bradford was baptized here in 1589 – the font reputed to have been used at the time of Bradford is still in the church, having been rescued from a local farm where it was being used as a water trough for the animals. The building dates back to AD 1080 and a stained glass window depicts Bradford's journey to the New World. There are other interesting features in this ancient building which can often be found open during the week.

Holland – Leiden Pilgrim Museum

9 Beschuitsteeg (Biscuit) Alley, Leiden

The Leiden American Pilgrim Museum is situated in a house built around 1370 and contains a collection of objects from the times of the Pilgrims – some of which belonged to the Pilgrims themselves. The Museum web site carries details of a walking tour of historic Leiden including the burial site of John Robinson in the Baptistery of the Pieterskirk.

Website: leidenamericanpilgrimmuseum.org

Above: Leiden Pilgrim Museum

Below: Detail from the doorway of St. Helena's Church Austerfield, where William Bradford was baptized

➋ All at sea

William Bradford recorded that the refugees in Leiden enjoyed, 'much sweet and delightful society and spiritual comfort together in the ways of God under the able ministry and prudent government of Mr John Robinson.' Sadly, it was not to last

The hope of religious freedom and a new uncomplicated life in Holland had proved transient. For many, the initial enthusiasm had faded, and the poor pay, menial work and harsh conditions took their toll. Others found the Dutch culture uncomfortable and the language impossible, leading some to return to England, preferring 'the prisons in England rather than this liberty in Holland with these afflictions.' The faithful Elder, William Brewster, set up a publishing house which became known as the Pilgrim Press and he was joined by a master printer named John Reynolds, who in turn brought out young Edward Winslow as an apprentice. The press produced tracts and pamphlets which were smuggled into England and, once discovered, brought the wrath of the king on to Brewster's head once again. King James gave orders that he be arrested but these were frustrated as Brewster went into hiding.

However the issue disturbed the peace of some within the congregation at Leiden. Many were also concerned about their children in the lax moral and spiritual climate of Holland and there was also concern that their families were becoming 'foreigners' as they grew up immersed in Dutch culture and language. It seemed that their goal had not yet been reached and they began looking elsewhere. What they really needed was a place where they could start completely afresh – and at that point in history it seemed as if the whole world was literally open to them. There were many possibilities and after much discussion a vote was taken which set their hearts towards Virginia – despite the fact that the Anglican church, whose influence they had tried so hard to escape, was already settled there!

In 1619, Deacon Robert Cushman and John Carver of the Leiden congregation went to London to seek an arrangement with the Virginia Company for transport to Virginia, and permission to settle there. The

Facing page: *The Dutch city of Leiden, with many buildings dating from the 17th century. According to William Bradford: 'A fair & bewtifull citie, and of a sweet situation'*

Company was in dire straits at the time and desperately in need of colonists, but they could not provide the free passage that the refugees needed. Thomas Weston from London approached the applicants with an offer that was too good to refuse.

Weston was a speculator who had contacts with many 'Merchant Adventurers' who were willing to invest in a new settlement in the colonies. However, their motives were financial rather than spiritual. A contract was made with Weston and a company he established for the purpose. Whilst many aspects of this contract were acceptable to the Leiden congregation, the ever treacherous Weston altered it at the last minute and a period of wrangling ensued in which some of the Leiden congregation pulled out of the arrangement. To offset this, the Adventurers in London signed up new colonists, regardless of their religious convictions. Weston angrily penalized the Leiden congregants who had refused to sign the amended contract and refused to subsidize their efforts further.

False starts and leaky ships

In June 1620 the *Mayflower* was chartered, along with a second ship – the sixty ton *Speedwell* which was purchased with a view to staying in the New World with the new colony. The *Speedwell* was in poor condition and needed extensive re-fitting, including new masts, larger than the original. Most likely these were to become responsible for the failure of the ship to reach New England. The strain produced on the ship's hull by the new masts caused the ship to leak and forced the emigrants to abandon their journey twice and then to abandon the ship altogether.

On 21 July 1620 the first would-be settlers made their way to Delft Haven to board the *Speedwell*. Pastor Robinson had decided not to travel, preferring to remain with the congregation at Leiden for the time being. He preached to them and prayed for them and 'with watrie cheeks commended them with mutual imbrases and many tears, they tooke their leaves one of another.'

The *Mayflower* was a 180 'tun' merchant vessel; this did

Below: Site of John Robinson's house, Leiden. Robinson studied theology at the university there and purchased a house at the Groene Port (Green Gate) of the Pieterskeirk

not refer to her total weight, but the number of 'tuns' (barrels or wine casks) which she could carry. She was about ninety feet long, twenty five feet across the beam, and twelve and a half feet deep. Although the *Mayflower* was used for all kinds of cargo, records of journeys to places like Bordeaux indicated that she was a 'sweet ship' used for carrying wine – spillages from wine casks neutralized the foul stench of cargo and rubbish which was common in other ships.

The Master, Christopher Jones – only naval ships had captains – was born into a seafaring family and lived at Harwich where his house still stands at 21 Kings Head Street. He owned one quarter of the *Mayflower* and was a skilled architect having previously designed and built a ship – the *Josian* which he named after his second wife. Documents show that Jones was in command of the *Mayflower* as early as 1609 and that he moved to Rotherhithe in London.

Above, left: Mayflower *public house, Rotherhithe, stands on the Thames at the place where the* Mayflower *was moored*

Above, right: *The* Mayflower *memorial, Southampton*

Left*: Christopher Jones' house, 21 Kings Head Street, Harwich. Jones was the Master of the* Mayflower

Facing page: *The embarkation of the Pilgrims by Robert Walter Weir. William Bradford is depicted at center, kneeling in the background, symbolically behind Governor John Carver (holding hat)*

The *Speedwell* drew into Southampton Harbour at the beginning of August 1620 and tied up alongside the *Mayflower* which had sailed from Rotherhithe for the rendezvous. On board the *Mayflower* were those recruited by the Merchant Adventurers for the journey to the new colony. Immediately there were disputes over money spent without proper accounting, and Thomas Weston made a further attempt to have the Leiden leaders sign a revised contract, but with no success. More money was spent on the *Speedwell* and this, together with harbour fees, necessitated the sale of belongings, food and stores which the travellers could ill afford to lose, especially as Weston kept his threat to advance them no more funds.

On 5 August both ships sailed from Southampton Harbour with about 120 passengers in total. It was soon obvious that the *Speedwell* was leaking to the point of threatening the safety of the ship and it was decided to put into Dartmouth where a further two weeks were lost whilst repairs were undertaken. A second attempt at the crossing was made but after travelling some 300 miles out to sea the skipper of the *Speedwell* reported that once again his ship was in danger and it was decided to turn back for Plymouth where the ship was abandoned. The trauma of these events caused about twenty people to abandon the project altogether which was a blessing as now everyone would have to travel on the *Mayflower* which was hardly fitted for passenger comfort.

Atlantic crossing

6 September 1620 saw the

Mayflower finally set sail from Plymouth, into the cold waters of the North Atlantic towards a most uncertain future and where, within six months, half the passengers would be dead. Memorials now stand on Southampton and Plymouth harbours commemorating the faltering starts of the Pilgrims.

The journey lasted sixty-five days, which was not unreasonable for the time and, apart from sea-sickness in the early days, was relatively incident free given the crowded conditions on board the vessel. The most notable events were firstly that a crew member: 'a proud and very profane young man' who had antagonized the passengers greatly, died half way through the journey; this was seen as a token of God's judgment on him. Secondly, one of the passengers, John Howland, fell overboard ; he managed to catch hold of a rope trailing from the ship and was hauled back on board. Having survived this near tragedy, Howland went on to have ten children with his wife Elizabeth and eighty eight grandchildren. The house occupied by his son Jabez can be seen at 33 Sandwich Street, Plymouth (MA). Howland is buried on Burial Hill in Plymouth and his headstone records that he was 'a Godly man and an ancient professor of the ways of Christ'.

For most of the journey, the passengers were crammed into the gun deck, otherwise called the 'tween' deck as it is the middle deck between the upper deck and the cargo hold below. The height of the tween deck was just 5 ½ feet and conditions were undoubtedly cramped and unsavoury, especially during the storms which marked part of the voyage. Only occasional bouts of fair weather would allow them onto the upper deck for fresh air and some respite from the conditions below.

Three of the women were heavily pregnant at the time of the voyage and there were about thirty young children,

Left: Mayflower *Memorial, The* Mayflower *Steps, Plymouth Harbour (UK)*

Right: *The Howland House, Plymouth (MA).* Mayflower *passengers John and Elizabeth Howland lived here with their son Jabez*

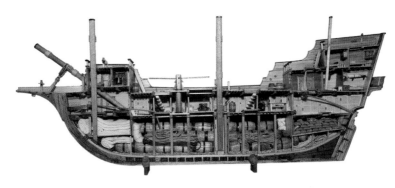

Above: *A section through a sixteenth century merchant ship*

including a one year old girl, Humility Cooper, an orphan in the company of her Aunt Ann (Cooper) Tilley. Ellen and Mary More, aged four and eight, were illegitimate children sent away by their (step) father Samuel to escape the shame of their mother's infidelity to him. Both girls died in the first winter. Family groups paid the ship's carpenter to construct small cabins with raised platforms for sleeping and storage of their meagre goods beneath. Even after their arrival at Cape Cod, the ship continued to be their home for some months. William and Susanna White's son Peregrine was born shipboard in Provincetown Harbour.

The intention of the Pilgrims, in accord with their charter, was to settle in the area of the Hudson River, in present day New York – although in 1620 it was considered part of the territory of Virginia. However, the ship approached the New England coastline far to the north and several attempts by the master to battle south were defeated due to the fierce tides and currents of the 'Pollack Rip' around Cape Cod. When the passengers realized they would have to settle for landing far from their agreed destination, discord arose between the Pilgrim settlers and the Adventurers (or 'Strangers' as they are sometimes called).

The Puritan Separatists had embarked on this venture with high spiritual ideals and priorities, but the financial necessities of the journey meant that they were already a mixed company, with about half of their number less than sympathetic to those ideals. Their essential differences were recognized as having potential for conflict and so it was decided that a form of covenant between the parties needed to be drawn up as the basis for the new settlement. This gave rise to what is known as the Mayflower Compact. Forty one of the male passengers signed the compact. In addition to this, John Carver was elected to be the Governor of the new colony. Carver had been instrumental, with Robert Cushman, in

Above: *The signing of the Mayflower Compact. Painting by Jean Leon Gerome Ferris*

The Text of the Mayflower Compact

'In the name of God, Amen. We, whose names are underwritten, the Loyal Subjects of our dread Sovereign Lord, King James, by the Grace of God, of England, France and Ireland, King, Defender of the Faith. Having undertaken for the Glory of God, and Advancement of the Christian Faith, and the Honour of our King and Country, a voyage to plant the first colony in the northern parts of Virginia; do by these presents, solemnly and mutually in the Presence of God and one of another, covenant and combine ourselves together into a civil Body Politick, for our better Ordering and Preservation, and Furtherance of the Ends aforesaid; And by Virtue hereof to enact, constitute, and frame, such just and equal Laws, Ordinances, Acts, Constitutions and Offices, from time to time, as shall be thought most meet and convenient for the General good of the Colony; unto which we promise all due submission and obedience. In Witness whereof we have hereunto subscribed our names at Cape Cod the eleventh of November, in the Reign of our Sovereign Lord, King James of England, France and Ireland, the eighteenth, and of Scotland the fifty-fourth. Anno Domini, 1620.'

obtaining the patent from the Virginia Company for the new colony.

The first landing

On Saturday 11 November 1620, after sixty-five days at sea, the crowded ship drew in to Provincetown Harbour (then called Cape Cod Harbour). The first impression of the harbour was that it could easily hold 'a thousand ships' and was protected on every side except from the north. Sixteen 'well-armed' men made the first journey ashore and on reaching land they 'fell upon their knees and blessed the God of heaven who had brought them over the vast and furious ocean and delivered them from all the perils and miseries thereof, again to set their feet on the firm and stable earth, their proper element' (Bradford). Not only did the harbour provide much needed protection from the open sea, there was a plentiful supply of fresh food in the form of shellfish, ducks, geese and other fowl. The passengers were also amazed to see countless whales frolicking in the seas in and around the Cape. The next day was the Sabbath and the whole company gave the day to worship, rest and prayer.

The *Mayflower* carried a 'shallop' (a flat bottomed boat) in four sections with the intention of re–assembling them for use when the new lands were reached. However, the rough journey had taken its toll on the boat and it would be several days before the carpenter was able to make it seaworthy. In the meantime, an overland exploration was

Top: *Pilgrim's memorial marking the first landing of the* Mayflower *in Provincetown, New England on 11 November 1620*

Above: *The shallop –* Mayflower II

undertaken, with Captain Miles Standish in charge. The small group made their way south down the Cape's spine and had their first sight of the Native People – about six plus a dog. On seeing the visitors they ran for the woods, and although pursued, were not to be seen again. The following morning they discovered the first fresh water at a place which became known as Pilgrims' Spring.

The party discovered evidence of Native graveyards as well as debris, including the remnants of a fort, which reminded them that they were not the first to travel to this land. At a location now known as 'Corn Hill' they came across an area of sand which had recently been smoothed out. They dug down and found a reed basket filled with dried corn as well as corn still on the cob. These stores, used by the Native Peoples, could stay viable for months and even years. The explorers decided to take these to supplement their meagre supply of provisions for planting in the new settlement, seeing the provision of this as divinely ordained for their future survival. William Bradford records that they fully intended to give the Natives 'full satisfaction' for the supplies when they met with them, and indeed did so some months later. Shortly afterwards, Bradford stepped into a deer trap and found himself swinging by the leg in considerable pain but wholly impressed by the ingenuity of the Natives.

Exploring the new land

A further expedition was launched on 27 November under the leadership of Christopher Jones using the newly completed shallop. Thirty–four men took part and their first destination was at what is now called Pilgrim Lake. Travelling south to a point they named Cold Harbour (Pamet Harbour – modern Truro) they encountered severe weather, with six inches of snow falling overnight. They arrived at a place called Corn Hill and searched through the deep snow to secure more of the Native's corn stores; Jones gladly returned to the

Mayflower with these freshly acquired supplies.

Standish and others remained to further explore the peninsula, during which time they discovered some mounds and dug them up to discover Native graves. They also saw some Native houses, apparently abandoned in a hurry, from which various items which might be of future value to them were taken. Bradford and Winslow recorded,

'The houses were made with long young sapling trees, bended and both ends stuck into the ground. They were made round, like unto an arbor, and covered down to the ground with thick and well wrought mats, and the door was not over a yard high, made of a mat to open. The chimney was a wide open hole in the top, for which they had a mat to cover it close when they pleased.... we found wooden bowls, trays and dishes, earthen pots, handbaskets made of crabshells wrought together, also an English pail or bucket.... There was also baskets of sundry sorts, bigger and some lesser, finer and some coarser; some were curiously wrought with black and white in pretty works, and sundry other of their household stuff. We found also two or three deer's heads, one whereof had been newly killed, for it was still fresh. There was also a company of deer's feet stuck up in the houses, harts' horns, and eagles' claws, and sundry such like things there was, also two or three baskets full of parched acorns, pieces of fish, and a piece of a broiled herring."

The third 'discovery' was undertaken on 6 December with the intention of exploring the bay further afield and seeking a suitable site for settlement. The *Mayflower*'s pilots, Coppin and Clark headed the expedition, along with fourteen others including William Bradford. As they turned into Wellfleet

Below: Cape Cod seashore. The Pilgrims landed at the beginning of a harsh New England winter season and soon even the beaches would be deep in snow

Bay they came upon a dozen Natives cutting up the carcass of a whale on the beach. The Natives fled, taking whatever whale flesh they could carry with them. The settlers camped on the beach overnight only to be attacked by the Natives the next dawn, with a hail of arrows. The settlers used their muskets and all escaped injury as their assailants disappeared into the woods.

Explorations around the vast bay westwards and northwards towards Plymouth continued, setting foot at first on Clark's Island to the north of Plymouth. Having observed the Sabbath day, they stepped ashore at Plymouth although, despite persistent stories concerning the famous 'Plymouth Rock', none of the records make mention of any particular rock as being the place of landing on this occasion. Plymouth Bay was a vast improvement on the shores of Cape Cod, with freshwater brooks, springs and cornfields. The Discoverers returned to the *Mayflower* with reports of their journey to find that William Bradford's wife, Dorothy, had fallen overboard and drowned in the icy waters whilst they were absent. The evidence implies that this was no more than a tragic accident, although popular films

Below: The Pilgrims' discovery of Cape Cod in 1620/21

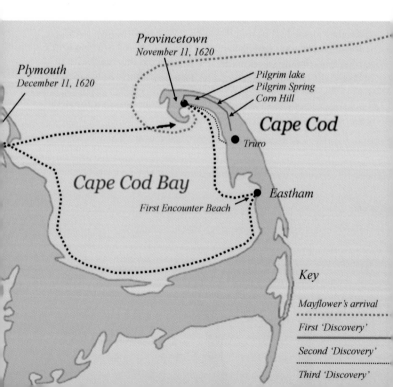

Right: First
Encounter Beach
near modern day
Eastham, where
the Pilgrims saw a
group of Natives
cutting up a
whale carcass

and books have helped to sustain the myth that her death was suicide brought on by depression.

'The Great Sickness'

In the following days the ship's surgeon, Giles Heale, was undoubtedly stretched to the limit of his medical abilities as several more succumbed to scurvy and fevers. Heale's duties would also have included that of ship's barber, but we might assume he had little time for this as half of the company died from the 'Great Sickness' before he returned to England and took up a practice in Drury Lane. One of the passengers, Isaac Allerton, gave Heale a copy of *Annotations Upon the Psalms* by Henry Ainsworth. This book can be seen at the Library of Virginia in Richmond. Another passenger, Dr Samuel Fuller, was described as the surgeon and physician to the Pilgrims by William Bradford. His apprentice, a young man by the name of William Butten, had been sick most of the journey and died just off the coast of New England. His name is among the list of names on a memorial at Provincetown, commemorating those who died on the *Mayflower* either at sea or whilst in Cape Cod Harbour.

William Bradford writes movingly of 'six or seven sound persons' among them who tirelessly ministered to the sick and dying in those early days. They 'spared no pains night or day... dressed them meat (prepared food), made their beds, washed their loathsome clothes – in a word did all the homely and necessary offices for them which dainty and queasy stomachs cannot endure to hear named.' Amongst these, Bradford specifically mentions the loving service of Elder William Brewster and Myles Standish towards their suffering brethren – himself included.

INFORMATION

Plymouth (UK)

Just off the harbour there is a small Mayflower Museum with interactive displays showing the development of the harbour from a natural rocky shelter to the modern attraction it is today. The Pilgrims Point Archway leads to a suspended platform over the water, around which a decorative handrail illustrates the Mayflower's journey. The original 'Mayflower Steps' from where the passengers re-embarked the ship are lost to the developing harbour but the Admiral MacBride public house at 1 The Barbican claims to be built over them.

3-5 The Barbican, Plymouth, PL1 2LR
Website: Mayflower Museum, Plymouth UK

London

The Mayflower public house at 117 Rotherhithe Street in London stands on the site of The Shippe public house, near to where the Mayflower was docked and from which it set off to join the Speedwell at Southampton in July 1620. Christopher Jones is buried in the nearby St Mary's churchyard where a memorial to him stands in the grounds. A few hundred

yards east along the Thames Pathway is a statue entitled 'Sunbeam Weekly and the Pilgrim's Pocket'. The statue by Peter McClean depicts a young boy of the 1930's reading a newspaper account of the Mayflower's journey whilst a Pilgrim character looks over the boy's shoulder – amazed at the changes in the world since their pioneering journey.

Harwich (UK)

The home of the Mayflower's Master, Christopher Jones still stands at 21 Kings Head Street.

In George Street the Harwich Mayflower Project is building a sea going replica of the Mayflower, expected to be completed in time for a 400th anniversary transatlantic voyage in 2020. The charity behind the project teaches traditional skills and offers apprenticeships through which the town has benefitted from a refurbished rail station and rail shed.

Website - harwichmayflower.com

Provincetown (MA)

Modern day Provincetown would shock those Pilgrims who first stepped ashore here in 1620. Now much renowned for its liberal values it is as far from the ideals of the godly settlers as could be imagined. In 1910 a monument was unveiled in the town to mark the arrival of the settlers.

Pilgrim Memorial (Provincetown)

The 77 metres tall structure dominates the town from High Pole Hill Road and at its top is 350 feet above sea level. A plaque commemorates the Mayflower Compact and the landing, and a museum documents Provincetown's history together with artefacts of Native American life.

HARWICH, UK

Christopher Jones'
House
Kings Head Street

THE QUAY

KINGS HEAD STREET

CHURCH STREET

Harwich
Mayflower
Project

GEORGE STREET

A120

Left: Sign for Harwich Mayflower Project

Right: Newly laid keel of the replica Mayflower, Harwich, UK

③ A safe haven

The Mayflower and her passengers relocated to the harbour at Plymouth on 16 December 1620 and it was determined that houses should be built on what is now Cole's Hill. On 25 December, the frame of the first house was erected

A few days later, at the top of the hill, a rudimentary fort was erected for the cannons from the ship. Plans were made for the construction of a town but the ravages of illness reduced the workforce – and the need for housing – drastically. The infant colony worked hard to establish itself but the death toll grew, with several families completely wiped out. In the first few months of the expedition 52 people perished. The ordeal of the sea journey, the harsh winter conditions on their arrival, and malnutrition all took a heavy toll on the newly arrived settlers. Whilst there was abundant food in the sea, many were farmers and few had the skills needed to catch fish; it would be some time before any crops could be sown.

A short walk down the harbour front from *Mayflower II*, under a Roman style portico, sits the rock known as Plymouth Rock. More symbolic than historical, this rock has a dubious but colourful history. Although none of the contemporary records of the settlers ever mentions such a landmark, in 1741 Thomas Faunce, then 94 years old, insisted that his father John (who arrived in the colony aboard the *Anne* in 1623) and several other *Mayflower* settlers had identified the rock to him as the very place they landed. In 1744, the rock Faunce had identified was split in two and one portion was taken to the Plymouth Town meeting-house and from there to Pilgrim Hall in 1834. In 1880 the two portions were again reunited on the waterfront and the date 1620 was carved into it.

Above: *Memorial (and tomb) of the* Mayflower *dead on Coles Hill, Plymouth (MA)*

Facing page: *Town Brook and Park – the site of the first settlement at Plymouth (MA)*

Above: *'Plymouth Rock'. A short walk down the harbour front from* Mayflower II, *under a Roman style portico, sits the rock known as Plymouth Rock, more symbolic than historical*

On these various journeys, the rock diminished in size and parts of it were taken to other sites. In 1920 the waterfront was redesigned and the rock was protected by the Romanesque canopy which stands today.

On 5 April 1621 Christopher Jones sailed the *Mayflower* back to England, arriving in Rotherhithe on 6 May. The arrival of the ship in London did not please the investors, especially Thomas Weston, as it returned empty. The plan had been to bring trading goods which could be sold to defray the costs to the investors. Instead of a rich hoard of furs and other valuable items, the ships hold was ballasted with stones from Plymouth Harbour! The absence of trading goods was ascribed by Weston to the 'selfishness' of the Pilgrims and to John Carver in particular. Christopher Jones would be dead within a year and the *Mayflower* rotted away at her mooring, not far from her Master's grave in St Mary's church. Some mystery surrounds the final resting place of the ship's timbers but a farm at Jordans Village in Buckinghamshire has become a place of pilgrimage for *Mayflower* descendants who believe that the ship's timbers were used to construct a barn on the property. Part of the difficulty is that there were around thirty vessels of the same name around this time, including one which sailed to the new Plymouth colony in 1629 carrying some members of the original Leiden congregation. This 'second' *Mayflower* made the Atlantic crossing on several occasions until 1641 when it disappeared with 140 passengers on board bound for Virginia.

The Native People

The structure of American Native society was hierarchical, with a nation divided into tribes, bands and clans. In addition to the 'Sachems' (chiefs) there were 'Pniese' (pronounced pa-NEES) who were specially trained fighters and 'Powwows' who were spiritual leaders. The southern Massachusetts area was the territory of the Wampanoag nation whose major tribes were the Pokanoket and the Nausets. The name Wampanoag means 'People of the first light'. The tribes were headed by a Sachem, and Massasoit was the great Sachem of the Wampanoag nation. The religious aspect of Native life was complex, with tribal variations and principles passed orally from generation to generation. Their belief system would not be readily identified or understood by those from outside, least of all by Western people with neatly packaged ideas of religion. They were conscious of a supernatural power, or being, and there were creation stories which explained the origins of the tribe. Nature and animals were of great symbolic significance. Religious observance centred around feasts and ceremonies which had little relevance outside the tribe. Perhaps it is best to describe them as 'spiritual' rather than religious, with every aspect of life having spiritual as well as practical implications.

Even before 1620, relationships between Europeans and the Native peoples had been severely strained. The Nausets had suffered at the hands of Captain Hunt who, on an expedition in 1614 with Captain John Smith of Pocahontas fame abducted about 20 of their number for sale as slaves in Europe. Consequently, three years later, a French ship visiting the region was besieged and most of its crew were killed in an attack motivated by revenge. However, before the end of the decade visiting Europeans had unleashed a far more dangerous enemy on the area – disease. When the 1620 Pilgrims arrived they found a seriously reduced Native community and several tribal

Top: St Mary's Church, Rotherhithe – the place of Christopher Jones' burial

Above: Memorial to Christopher Jones the captain of the Mayflower, St Mary's Church, Rotherhithe, England

Centre: A Wampanoag Native in traditional dress at the Plimoth Plantation. There were several variants of the original spelling for the more modern Plymouth. The Plantation adopted this variant to distinguish it from the modern city

villages had been completely devastated by measles and smallpox which the Natives believed to be the result of supernatural powers possessed by the settlers.

Welcome Englishmen!

In the middle of March 1621 a Native appeared at a location known as Watson's Hill. There had been several such sightings but on this occasion the lone character walked towards the town and to the great surprise of the guards sent out to meet him said, 'Welcome Englishmen'. His name was Samoset and he had learned his broken English from the fleets of fishermen which had visited Maine. He told them that the chief of the tribes in that region was a Sachem named Massasoit.

Some days after this first encounter, Samoset returned to the town with other Natives including one named Squanto. Squanto (also called Tisquantum) spoke fluent English and it was discovered that he had even lived in the Corn Hill area of London! He had been captured by the English trader Thomas Hunt in 1614 and taken to Spain and was rescued from being sold into slavery by some friars who introduced him to Christianity. They allowed him to attempt a journey home and he first found his way to London where he lived for a while with a shipbuilder. He eventually made his way back to New England in 1619 where he discovered that many of his fellow Natives had succumbed to disease. Squanto's knowledge of the environment and Native

Pocahontas

Pocahontas was the daughter of Powhatan, the chief of an alliance of Alonquian tribes at Tidewater in Virginia. In 1607, Captain John Smith arrived at the trading post at Jamestown and whilst exploring the region was captured by the tribe and taken to Powhatan. Smith wrote several accounts of his experience, but in one he spoke of his imminent death at the hands of Powhatan when Pocahontas intervened by placing her own head in the way of her father's club. Smith was released and eventually returned to England. Pocahontas continued to mediate between her people and the English, even bringing them food when their state became perilous. When war finally broke out between the settlers and the Natives, Pocahontas was lured aboard an English ship and held hostage until Powhatan released English captives and weapons. During her prolonged captivity, she converted to the Christian faith under the ministry of Alexander Whitaker and was subsequently baptized, taking the Christian name 'Rebecca'. Pocahontas declined to return to her father and instead married John Rolfe and travelled with him to England in 1616 where she was shown as an example of the effect of the gospel in the New World.

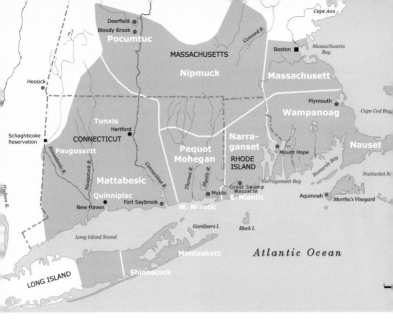

practices were to save the settlers from certain starvation. He showed them that seed needed to be planted with fish (as fertiliser) otherwise it would not grow. His insight into the structure and thinking of Native society would also prove invaluable and he was no doubt a gift from the Lord to the settlers at that time.

Massasoit was the Sachem of the Pokanoket tribe but was also chief of a confederacy of Wampanoag Natives. His actual name was Ousamequin. Through the mediation of Samoset and Squanto, Massasoit entered the settlement and met with their representatives, including the Governor, John Carver. At that meeting, a formal agreement was drawn up in which the parties agreed to do each other no harm and specified the consequences of any breach. It has to be said that

Top: *Map showing the territories of Southern New England tribes about 1600*

Above: *Head Of Squanto L. Gaugen: Wood, textured paint. In 1880, a wooden sculpture showing the landing of the Pilgrims was placed in the pediment over Pilgrims Hall Museum's front entrance. The figures were removed in 1909. This wooden head of the Native American Squanto is the only surviving piece*

Above: Proudly overlooking the harbour at Plymouth is a striking statue of the Pokanoket 'Great' Sachem, Massasoit

that he could not overcome them and therefore needed to enter into a form of peaceful relationship. For over forty years Massasoit's presence ensured relative stability in relationships with the Native community even though the English tested this allegiance to its limits at times by the uneven conditions they often imposed on Massasoit's people. However, after his death some time between 1660–62 the uneasy peace collapsed as his second son Metacomet (known as 'King Philip'), was convinced that the English had murdered his older brother Wamsutta. This would bring to a climax tensions which had long been mounting and would result in the terrible period known as King Philip's war (see chapter 6).

In April 1621 Governor Carver collapsed suddenly whilst out working in the fields, complaining of terrible pains in his head. He was carried back to the town, unconscious and died a few days later. William Bradford then became Governor of the colony – a position he would hold for a total of over thirty years.

Although there is no doubt that Squanto was a real benefit to the English settlers, teaching them native skills and the means of raising crops and food, it is clear that he also attempted to play both sides against each other to his own advantage. At one point Massasoit became so angry with Squanto because of his treachery, that he demanded Squanto be handed over to be put to death in accordance with the agreement between the Natives and the

the agreement is rather biased against the Natives who were required to make wider promises than the English. They would also discover that the English were much less prepared to adhere to its conditions than they insisted for the Natives. Massasoit returned to his camp but Squanto remained with the English and began to make himself indispensable to them.

Massasoit's aid to the settlers in the early years was also crucial to their survival. He had observed their arrival and was initially ill disposed towards them due to a number of bad experiences with English speaking traders in the past. He was, however, convinced

settlers. Squanto escaped on this occasion as Governor Bradford was so fond of him that he refused to hand him over, and the arrival of a boat in the bay proved to be a sufficient distraction to enable Bradford to delay his decision until the matter might be forgotten.

This further increased the tensions between the settlers and the Natives and there is speculation that Squanto's death late in 1622 may have been due to poisoning. He was with William Bradford on a trading expedition and was forced to shelter in Manamoyik Bay (near modern–day Chatham). Squanto's nose suddenly began to bleed and he recognised this as a sign of his imminent demise. He asked that Bradford pray for him so that he should go to the 'Englishman's God in heaven' and within a few days he was dead.

'We had a good increase'

Over the following months an uneasy peace prevailed between the settlers and the Natives, and several more Sachem from the surrounding tribes made alliances with the English and expressed loyalty to King James. The English began to trade goods they had brought for the Natives' furs and food. By late September or early October there was good reason to give thanks to God after the harvest and the abundance of fowl. The occasion most often referred to as the first 'Thanksgiving' saw both English and Native sitting down and sharing the fruits of nature's bounty together.

Massasoit and around ninety of the Natives joined in this feast which lasted three days. Edward Winslow wrote, 'And God be praised, we had a good increase…. Our harvest being gotten in, our governor sent four men on fowling so that we might after a special manner rejoice together….'

November 1621 saw the arrival of the *Fortune* in Plymouth Harbour, sent by the English investors and bringing another thirty-seven settlers to swell the depleted ranks of the colonists. Unfortunately, they arrived with virtually no food or provisions for the settlement and therefore

Above: *The statue of William Bradford in Plymouth Harbour. Bradford was five times Governor of Plymouth for 30 out of 35 years*

Above: The First Thanksgiving at Plymouth *by Jennie A. Brownscombe 1914*

Left: *A present day reconstruction of the defensive walls of the Plimoth Plantation*

the struggling settlers had to accommodate the new arrivals in their houses and feed them as well. The ship also carried a scathing letter from Thomas Weston lamenting their slow progress and the lack of return for the investors. In mid December the *Fortune* set sail for England, this time with a hold full of skins and oak the value of which should cut their debt in half. However, in a further blow to relationships between the settlers and investors, the ship was seized by the French on its return journey and none of the goods reached England.

Rumours of war

Tensions outside the little town of Plymouth grew as other Sachem became envious of the relationship between the Pokanokets and the settlers. Canonicus, the Narangasset Sachem, sent the settlers an ominous bundle of arrows wrapped in rattlesnake skin. Governor Bradford sent it back filled with gunpowder and bullets in equally threatening fashion, but the need was felt to fortify the town with eight foot high fences around the entire perimeter. Tensions also continued inside the fence as Christmas Day came. The Adventurers insisted the day should be a religious holiday whilst the Christians, who did not observe the festival, continued to work. Governor Bradford allowed the Adventurers' request but insisted that the day be treated as a Sabbath. When he later found the Adventurers playing 'stoolball' he confiscated their equipment. The frivolous conduct of the Adventurers caused difficulty with the leadership and began to expose the fracture lines between the two very different groups which had found themselves thrown together in the extremity of the new colony.

One of the better-known characters on board the *Mayflower* was Miles Standish who had travelled to the new colony with his wife, Rose; she was sadly among those who did not make it beyond the first month of 1621. Standish's actual military career is unclear but he referred to himself as 'Captain' and took a prominent role in the exploration of the Cape and the defence of Plymouth. In the poem 'The Courtship of Miles Standish', Henry Wadsworth Longfellow reveals how the settlers hid their graves so that the Natives would not see how many had died.

"Yonder there, on the hill by the sea, lies buried Rose Standish;
Beautiful rose of love, that bloomed for me by the wayside!
She was the first to die of all who came in the Mayflower!
Green above her is growing the field of wheat we have sown there,

Shelling out

The white and purple tubular shells of whelks and clams from the North Atlantic coast had long been used by the Native Peoples to mark significant national and personal events. The shells were often woven into belts which were used as storytelling aids with the various shells marking significant events. Belts could be six feet in length and contain 6,000 shells, the wearing of which indicated power and importance. Shells were drilled and worked on a grinding stone into smooth, glossy tubes. In time these also came to mark transactions and to be used in purchasing pelts and other goods from the Natives. Their

value was determined by their colour and rarity, with purple quahog (clam) shells considered the most valuable. Six white or three black shells were worth one penny. In New England, these shells, called wampum, became legal tender between 1637–1661 but the availability of the shells to the coastal communities of settlers and the introduction of metal tools resulted in over use and devaluation.

Until the late 1700's it was possible to pay for tuition at Harvard College with wampum. The modern American slang terms for money, 'clams', and the phrase 'shelling out' derive from the use of wampum.

Pictured: *Wampum – shells of whelks and clams were used to mark significant events in Native People's history but eventually came to be used as currency*

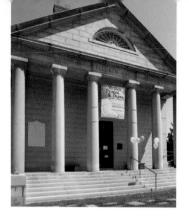

Above: *Pilgrim Hall Museum, Plymouth (MA) houses a large collection of Pilgrim artefacts and records*

> *Better to hide from the Indian scouts the graves of our people,*
> *Lest they should count them and see how many already have perished!"*

The boat which had proved a distraction and saved Squanto's life was from a ship which had been hired by Thomas Weston, the chief agent to the investors in the UK. It transpired that Weston had betrayed the Mayflower Pilgrims and decided to establish his own settlement about 25 miles north of Plymouth at Wessagusset (Weymouth). Not only did Weston intend to compete with the Plymouth Pilgrims for trade, but he sent his advance party of around sixty to Plymouth to be looked after, fed and sheltered whilst a suitable site could be found. Weston's mercenary approach to the venture meant that he discouraged families from taking the journey and instead sent mostly single men (many reputed to be of dubious character)

who he hoped would have the strength and determination to make a success of the settlement. Historian Charles Francis Adams, Jr describes Weston as having a 'brain teemed with schemes for deriving sudden gain from the settlement of the new continent.' The newcomers struggled to make a success of their commission and there were repeated accusations between the Natives and the Weymouth settlers about theft and unfavourable trading terms. Despite the relatively plentiful supply of food, the Weymouth settlers seemed unable to make the most of it and began to starve.

In March 1623 rumours were rife that the Natives intended to slaughter all those in the Weymouth colony as a result of their double-dealings. Massasoit, grateful to Edward Winslow for nursing him though a bout of terrible sickness, told him that several tribes were conspiring to attack both settlements, and he encouraged them to make the first strike. Governor Bradford called on Miles Standish to organize the defence of the two settlements and he went to Weymouth with a small group of men, intending to take the initiative and mount a pre–emptive strike on the Natives. Standish arranged a meeting with two of the suspected protagonists, Wituwamat and Pecksuot , and when they had begun to eat a meal, the settlers turned on the Natives and slaughtered them with their own knives. The violence spread to the nearby village where several other Natives were also killed.

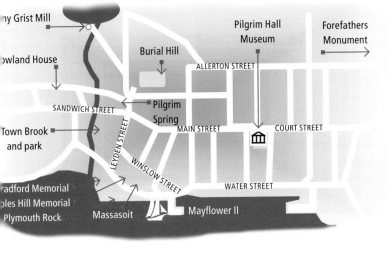

Above: Map of Plymouth (MA) Pilgrim Highlights

Below: Mayflower II sits in pride of place on Plymouth waterfront

TRAVEL INFORMATION

Pilgrim Hall Museum

75 Court Street
The oldest museum in the United States, containing a variety of artefacts, artwork and documents telling the story of the Mayflower settlers. Among the exhibits are a chair belonging to Elder William Brewster and the cradle of Peregrine White who was born to William and Susanna White aboard the Mayflower shortly after they had arrived.
  Website: pilgrimhallmuseum.org

Mayflower II

State Pier, Plymouth (MA)
The replica ship Mayflower II, now sits in Plymouth Harbour. Built in Brixham, Devon (UK). She is the result of a collaboration between an Englishman, Warwick Charlton, and the Plimoth Plantation Museum. After a few years of planning and negotiation, the work began in 1955 using traditional methods and materials, based on plans already drawn up by Plimoth Plantation. The ship is part of the Plimoth Plantation Museum and visitors can go on board, experience the claustrophobic conditions and talk to the experts who recreate characters from the crew of the original journey.
  Website: plimoth.org

1620. The park contains the Jenney Grist Mill, a replica of the mill built by John Jenney in 1636, and statues and sculpture commemorating the Pilgrims.

Website: plimoth.org/mill

Burial Hill

Leiden Street
This cemetery holds the graves of several notable Pilgrims including Governor William Bradford, John Howland, William Brewster as well as Mary Allerton Cushman who outlived all the Mayflower passengers, dying in 1699 at the age of 83 having had 8 children and 50 grandchildren. Also on the hill is a memorial to the Burma missionary Adoniram Judson who lived in the town at the beginning of the 1800's and whose house is still standing at 17 Pleasant Street.

Howland House

33 Sandwich Street
The Howland house claims to be the only house remaining in Plymouth in which Pilgrim settlers from the Mayflower actually lived. John Howland, who escaped death after being washed overboard, went on to have ten children and lived to the age of eighty. One of his sons, Jabez, owned the house; John and his wife also lived there for a time.
Website: pilgrimjohnhowlandsociety.org

The National Monument to the the Forefathers

Allerton Street
This colossal granite monument was completed in 1888 after almost sixty years of planning and construction. The sculpture is octagonal in design and faces north east towards the harbour and in the general direction of Plymouth England. The central character of the statue is 'Faith' and she holds her right hand towards heaven and clutches a Bible in her left.

Cole's Hill Memorial

This is the location of the first cemetery for the Pilgrims and in 1920 remains of those buried here were collected and interred in the memorial.

Town Brook and Park

Spring Lane
Town Brook runs through the centre of Plymouth and through a park known as Brewster Gardens, covering an area allocated to Elder William Brewster in

Harlow Old Fort House

119 Sandwich Street
The fort on Burial Hill was dismantled
at the end of King Philips War in 1677
and Sergeant William Harlow was
given permission to use its timbers to
construct the house. In 1920 the Plymouth
Antiquarian Society purchased the
property and it now functions as a living
museum.
Website: plymouthantiquariansociety.org

For walking tours of historical
downtown Plymouth conducted by
Native American guides see www.
nativeplymouthtours.com

Plimoth Plantation

137 Warren Avenue, Plymouth MA 02360
Not far to the south is Plimoth Plantation,
a faithful interpretation of the first
township established by the settlers on
what is now known as Leiden Street in
nearby Plymouth. Visitors can experience
life in a traditional Wampanoag village
and talk to Native People (a term preferred
to 'Indians' when talking to the guides)
from the Wampanoag or other Native
Nations who now work here as guides.
They do not play characters but speak from
a modern perspective about Native history
and culture.

From the Wampanoag village visitors
pass through the gates of the pallisaded
settlement and find themselves in the
Plymouth of 1627. Costumed guides
engage in conversations in the character
of the settlers and it is possible to visit
several houses and catch a glimpse of daily
life for the settlers. High on the hill at the
top of the village stands the fort which
doubles as the meeting house for civil and
religious meetings.

Website: plimoth.org

Top: William Bradford's grave, Burial
Hill Plymouth

Middle: Wampanoag Village scene,
Plimoth Plantation

④ The tide turns

The treacherous murder of Wituwamat and Pecksuot broke for ever the delicate balance of peace between the Natives and the settlers

Standish returned to Plymouth where he displayed the head of Wituwamat on the fort roof. Panic spread amongst the tribes and many fled to the wilderness where, in the following months, several of the most prominent Sachems died. The Settler/Native relationship was now changed for ever. Massasoit was regarded as a traitor by many of his own people. Despite this, he rose to prominence among the Wampanoag people in the power vacuum created by the demise of so many Sachem.

Back in Leiden, Pastor Robinson heard of Standish's attack on the Natives and mourned over it. He wrote to Governor Bradford: 'Oh how happy a thing it had been if you had converted some before you killed any.' He knew Standish from his time in Leiden, believing that he lacked Christian grace, and the slaughter of the Natives confirmed his deep mistrust. Robinson never fulfilled his stated intention to join the settlers in Plymouth, dying in Leiden in 1625. Even though he was so far away, this was a great blow to the Leiden faithful who had never had a pastor in the New World. William Brewster was their Elder in spiritual matters but they mourned the loss of the man they had always regarded as their true pastor.

By the time of Robinson's death, over a quarter of the original surviving Plymouth settlers had defected – either returning to England or moving to

Above: Native crafts at Plimoth Plantation

Facing page: The (reconstructed) fort at Plimoth Plantation. This also served as the meeting house for Christian worship and also functioned as the 'town hall'

Above: Native scrimshaw (carving) decoration on bone. Plimoth Plantation

and many wanted to turn back for England immediately. Some 'fell a-weeping, fancying their own misery in what they now saw in others; some pitying the distress they saw' (Bradford). The colonists' clothing was ragged and some were half naked, the only food being available was lobster (considered a lowly food due to its abundance) or a piece of fish. Hopes were further dashed when a drought came between May and the middle of July, scorching the soil and ruining the corn crop.

Sensing the Lord's displeasure upon them, the colony declared a day of prayer and humiliation. On the evening of the solemn day, a gentle rain fell and soaked the earth. The immediate effect on the crops was obvious as withered plants quickly revived. Even the Natives were astonished at this. The day gave way to much rejoicing in the Lord's mercy towards them and these events were undoubtedly a turning point in the viability of the colony. The resultant harvest was divided among the settlers for their individual use, and plots of land set apart for each family. The 'common course' (communal) approach to production of crops was now dissolved and each family was responsible for their own harvest. The effect of this was to turn corn into a more valuable commodity – being 'more precious than silver'. Families which had previously been careless in fields whilst working for everybody's benefit, became ardent farmers when faced with their own interest in the crop and the potential for

Virginia. The investors in London abandoned their support for the colony and several of the settlers themselves, including William Bradford, agreed to take on the outstanding debt. Although trade with the Natives began to thrive, with the newly discovered wampum acting in the place of money, the debt never seemed to diminish no matter how many furs, beaver pelts and how much wood was sent back to England on the steady flow of ships now making the journey to and from the New World.

A miracle witnessed

The supply ship *Anne* arrived at Plymouth in the summer of 1623 carrying a further sixty passengers to strengthen the colony. They found a shocking scene in which the harsh realities of the venture became clear to them

trade that it presented. Thus the economic stimulus for the colony had been discovered.

The Weymouth colony collapsed early the same year, 1623, with many returning to England but some joined the Plymouth community – adding to its woes. Thomas Weston arrived only to discover his venture had already failed and he eventually made for Virginia. A further attempt to revive Weymouth was made by Robert Gorges later the same year. After the efforts made by the Separatists to escape the clutches of the established church, Gorges brought two Anglican clergymen with him. This venture was also short lived and in the spring of 1624 it collapsed. The *Anne* sailed to England with its hold full of clapboard and Edward Winslow as a passenger. Winslow returned to Plymouth in 1624 on the *Charity* with three cows and a bull – the first of their kind in the New World.

Wolves in shepherd's clothing

In 1624, the first ordained minister, the Anglican Rev John Lyford, arrived at Plymouth aboard the *Charity*. He appeared to be a man of great humility and the settlers were impressed by his humble confessions of previous wrongdoings and of his passionate desire to be united with them in their spiritual quest. He was warmly welcomed among them as a brother in the Separatist cause. However, all was not what it seemed. Lyford's sympathies were with the established church and his previous wrongdoings were much more sordid than he

had been prepared to admit – including the rape of a young girl he had been counselling. Lyford became a thorn in the colonists' side and began writing letters back to England, disparaging the colony and its leaders. Governor Bradford, alerted by Lyford's suspicious conduct, took a shallop out to the ship and required the master to hand over Lyford's letters.

Confronted with his actions, Lyford appeared repentant

Below: Household gardens at the Plimoth Plantation

Bottom: A wooden house frame at Plimoth Plantation

but immediately wrote a fresh batch of complaints. He was supported in his campaign against the Plymouth leaders by John Oldham who had arrived on the *Anne* in 1623 from Derbyshire. The two men carried on a whispering campaign and drew several other discontents to them. When Oldham was confronted by Captain Standish, he rashly drew a knife on the soldier who, to match his short stature, was known to have a very short fuse. Oldham and Lyford were charged with 'plotting against them and disturbing their peace, both in respects of their civil and church state' and banished from the colony. Lyford appeared to show remorse and was briefly allowed a reprieve until this also was shown to be a sham. Oldham attempted to return to Plymouth and was swiftly marched to the shore by Miles Standish and a group of soldiers who each gave him a 'bob upon the bumme' with the butt of their muskets. Despite this, Oldham fared well, planting his own settlement at Nantasket, successfully engaging in trade with the Natives, and was even sent as a deputy to the General Court at Massachusetts in 1632.

Some of Lyford's letters had, however, reached the Adventurers in England and they were so dismayed by the reports that most wished to dissolve the company. Robert Cushman managed to persuade a few to hold on and a new arrangement to pay the outstanding debt of £1400 was agreed. The ship *Charity* was sent to Plymouth, full of goods to be sold to the colonists for the benefit of the Merchant Adventurers. The *Charity* returned to England full of fish, along with the *Little James*.

The *Little James* had been sent to fish in the waters off the Maine Coast but sank with the loss of the Master and some crew. She was re-floated to carry fish and

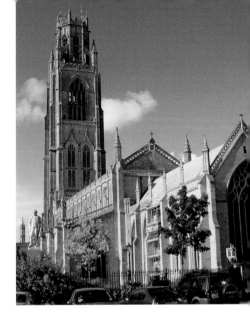

Left: View of the bay from Plimoth Plantation

Right: St Botolph's Church 'The Stump' Boston (Lincs) where John Cotton was minister. Cotton was driven to the colonies by the attempts of William Laud to prosecute him for his Separatist views

beaver pelts to England to pay off some £277 of the outstanding debt. Tragedy would strike once more, however, and she was attacked in the English Channel by Barbary pirates who carried the ship and her contents away to Morocco where the passengers and crew were sold as slaves. The loss of the *Little James* brought the Adventurers to the brink of bankruptcy. Isaac Allerton, on one of his regular visits to England to represent the Pilgrims affairs, negotiated a further deal with the merchants to surrender all rights to the colony for the sum of £1800 to be paid in nine annual instalments. Allerton would not always prove to be such a reliable agent and would, in fact, render the settlers with even greater debts due to his own double–dealing.

'Of all men.. I envy Mr Cotton of Boston'

As the Plymouth colony struggled to establish itself, the deepening conflict in England between non–conformists and state provided the necessary impetus for a further wave of disaffected believers to make their way to the shores of New England, amongst whom was John Cotton.

Born in 1584 in Derby, England, he received a theological education at Trinity College, Cambridge and was deeply affected by the preaching of the Puritan Richard Sibbes. In 1612, Cotton was ordained at St Botolph's Church in Boston (UK) and after a few years, began to discontinue various 'Anglican' practices. His non-conformity earned him a rebuke from the Bishop of Lincoln who described him as 'a young man unfit to be over such a factious people who was inclined with the Puritan spirit.' Cotton gained a reputation for simple but profound preaching and many were drawn to his ministry. Despite his reputation, his tenure at St Botolphs between

Left: *John Cotton, the much admired minister of Boston Lincolnshire. In his honour the city of Boston (MA) was named*

Right: *Anne Bradstreet plaque, Harvard University. Bradstreet was the first female poet published in England and New England. See also page 73*

Facing page, centre: *'Come over and help us'. The seal of the Massachusetts Bay Company*

1612 and 1632 largely escaped the sanctions meted out to those who failed to comply with the king's instruction concerning the forms of worship. Samuel Ward of Ipswich remarked, 'Of all men in the world I envy Mr. Cotton, of Boston, most; for he doth nothing in way of conformity, and yet hath his liberty, and I do everything that way, and cannot enjoy mine.'

At the departure of John Winthrop's company for New England in March 1630, Cotton preached a farewell sermon entitled 'God's Promise to His Plantation'. Two years later William Laud began to set him firmly in his sights and summoned him to appear before the court.

Cotton went into hiding where he formed the intention to leave England for the New World. His decision was not difficult to make as he preferred preaching in the New World to sitting in a 'loathsome prison'. Several of his contemporaries, including John Davenport, met with him and attempted to dissuade him from leaving, but during the discussions they too were convinced of its necessity and would themselves leave England shortly after. Cotton set sail on *The Griffin* in July 1633 and arrived at Trimountain in early September. His wife, Sarah, had given birth to a son on the journey and he was named 'Seaborn'. The town would later be renamed Boston in honour of Cotton's ministry there. He was ordained minister of the First Church in Boston later that year – a position he held until his death in 1652. Cotton was loved and highly respected both in England and New England alike. He was renowned for serious study, practical ministry and godliness. He was instrumental in shaping the colony's civil and ecclesiastical laws and his influence is regarded as largely responsible for the growing prominence of the Boston colony over Plymouth.

On moving to Sempringham, Lincolnshire in the mid 1620's, Puritans Thomas and Dorothy Dudley had come under the ministry of John Cotton at St Botolph's. The whole household travelled by covered wagon on weekends to hear Cotton preach. Their daughter, Anne, was born in 1612 and at the age of sixteen married Simon Bradstreet, a student of Emmanuel College Cambridge who was appointed by Thomas Dudley to be his aide in managing the affairs of the Earl of Lincoln. Bradstreet and his wife travelled with Dudley to the New World in 1630.

The Earl of Lincoln was sympathetic to the nonconformist cause, but fell foul of Charles I to whom he refused a loan and was subsequently thrown into the Tower of London. Charles increased pressure on the nonconformists and appointed William Laud, Bishop of London, to pursue a personal vendetta against the Puritan community. Faithful Puritans were therefore forced to consider fleeing the country. A wealthy couple – Lady Arbella married to Isaac Johnson, a wealthy Puritan preacher – met with Thomas Dudley, Thomas Hooker and Roger Williams at Sempringham. Their discussions resulted in the initiation of the Massachusetts Bay Company, which surprisingly received a charter from the king for the establishment of a new settlement north of the Plymouth colony. From Charles' point of view it was no doubt an opportunity to rid himself of some troublesome Puritans.

'Come over and help us!'

One of the principal aims of the Company was 'to win the natives of the country to the knowledge and obedience of the only true God and Saviour of mankind.' John Endecott was sent to prepare the way for further colonization of the region. His English roots are shrouded in mystery and Endecott was to become a controversial figure in the New England colony. He passionately held to Separatist Puritan principles but at times was merciless in his pursuit of purity. Endecott held the position of Governor of the Massachusetts Bay Colony for

sixteen years. He took a Separatist view of the church in contrast to John Winthrop who, though a nonconformist at heart, believed the Anglican church could still be reformed from within. Because of this, Endecott was willing to receive the banished Roger Williams when he was expelled from Boston (see end of this chapter) and even offered him a teaching post in the church at Salem.

John Winthrop was born into a wealthy family at Edwardstone, Suffolk in 1588. His father was a lawyer and owned considerable property as did his mother's family. He was trained at Trinity College, Cambridge, where his father was also a Director. His diary entries for the period show a passionate young man subject to intense inner struggles of a personal and spiritual nature. Winthrop became Lord of Groton Manor as well as an influential lawyer and member of the country's elite. In 1604 he married Mary Forth of Great Stambridge in Essex who bore him five children, the last two dying soon after birth. Mary herself succumbed to complications from the last birth and died in June 1615.

His period of mourning for Mary did not last long and by December 1615 he was married to Thomasine Clopton; however, tragedy was to strike once more and Thomasine died in childbirth a year later. In 1618 he married for the third time, to Margaret Tyndal of Great Maplestead in Essex and they lived at Groton when John was not in London. It is equally unclear when Winthrop became involved in the Massachusetts Bay Company's efforts but Charles' dissolution of Parliament, together with the persecution of Puritans and other nonconformists that followed, caused Winthrop to embrace the idea of emigration. His education and influence led the shareholders to persuade him to join them in the venture and voted him Governor, a position he would hold for twelve years during the first twenty years of the new colony.

Salem

The city of Salem was originally called Naumkeag, meaning 'fishing place' – referring to the Native People and the river at the location – and was founded by Roger Conant in 1626. Conant and

Below: The Arbella *(Arabella). Named after Lady Arbella who sponsored the Massachusetts Bay Colony enterprise*

Bottom: Salem historic waterfront

A city on a hill

Winthrop sailed aboard the *Arbella* with his two young sons but not his wife, who was pregnant and would join him later. Just before the departure – or perhaps even during the crossing, Winthrop delivered his sermon which included the reference to the settlers as a 'City on a hill' setting out the high ideals and strong faith which must mark the venture to the New England shores:

'For we must consider that we shall be as a City upon a Hill, the eies of all people are upon us; so that if we shall deal falsely with our God in this work we have undertaken and so cause him to withdraw his present help from us, we shall be made a story and a byword through the world, we shall open the mouths of enemies to speak evil of the ways of God and all professors for God's sake; we shall shame the faces of many of God's worthy servants, and cause their prayers to be turned into curses upon us till we be consumed out of the good land whether we are going.'

his wife and son had travelled from Devonshire (England) to Plymouth (MA) and later threw in their lot at Cape Ann some eighty miles to the north; they joined with the members of the Dorchester Company which hoped to capitalize on the bay's waters teeming with cod. The colony struggled with internal divisions and found it hard to make a profit from their fishing. Conant was keen to leave Plymouth as he did not fully share the Separatist position and was therefore happy to lead a small group to Naumkeag. In 1628, the arrival of John Endecott was welcomed by Conant who helped the settlers in their faltering attempts to establish a new colony.

Whilst they had proved inept at the business of fishing, the Cape Ann settlers had managed to build a two–storey house for their Governor, known as the 'Great House'. On his arrival, Endecott heard of the house and ordered that it be dismantled and brought to Naumkeag for his own use. The other settlers did not find life quite so comfortable and were forced to live in cramped, temporary lodges cut into the hillside or in Native style straw huts until they could afford the time and expense of constructing their own houses. Endecott's company also brought with them disease which quickly took its toll on the old and new settlers alike. Help was summoned from Plymouth who sent Deacon Samuel Fuller to minister to them in their sickness and to encourage them spiritually.

In 1630 the *Arbella* and three other ships sailed from the Isle of Wight and subsequently joined with others in a fleet totalling 11 ships. 700 men, women and children sailed on this expedition, together with 200 cattle, 60 horses and some goats; over half of the livestock perished on the journey.

On the arrival of the *Arbella* at Salem in June 1630, Winthrop and the Massachusetts Bay

Company settlers found their forerunners struggling to survive yet another harsh winter. Because of its exposed location Salem was soon deemed to be unsuitable for such an influx. In search of alternatives, Winthrop and Thomas Dudley sailed about 15 miles along the coast where they discovered many abandoned Native villages. They came to Mishawaum which had been taken over by a handful of earlier settlers and was now called Charlestown.

Above: Replica of the interior of the Governor's House at Pioneer Village

Top: A grass hut at Pioneer Village, the kind used by the settlers on their arrival in Salem

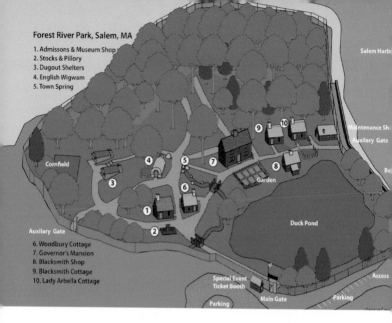

Above: *Map of Pioneer Village, Salem in 1630 showing the different house types used by the settlers on their arrival at Salem. (Pioneer Village map courtesy of George Courage www.georgecouragecreative.com)*

Winthrop decided that they would settle at this location, and a meeting house was soon erected. Being on a peninsula, the settlement was equally exposed to severe weather and the weakened travellers were barely able to cope with the harsh conditions leading to many deaths in the following months – including Lady Arbella and her husband. Because of the threat from Natives, it was also agreed that the settlers should disperse along the banks of the Charles River to avoid being concentrated in one place.

Realizing that the situation was serious, on 1 August Winthrop called on the faithful travellers to covenant together to uphold the high spiritual aims of the settlers to establish a 'City on a hill'. Charlestown also proving unsuitable, he directed that they move south, to a location on the Shawmut Peninsula known as Trimountain. Several refused to move, including Dudley and Bradstreet.

A meetinghouse was opened in Trimountain and the town later renamed Boston in honour of John Cotton. Those who remained in Charlestown had to travel the few miles there each Lord's Day for worship under the direction of John Wilson. This new settlement proved to be fertile and productive but it was too late for many and at least 200 had perished. Dudley was also forced to subdue his pride and move south. Along the Charles River he and others established a settlement known as Newe Towne, later to become Cambridge.

7 Rough seas

The English attacked the Natives mercilessly. Those who were not slaughtered were taken captive and many were sold as slaves for the Caribbean sugar plantations. John Eliot objected fiercely: 'To sell Indians away from all means of grace... is the way for us to be active in destroying their souls'

Governor Winslow's aide, Captain Benjamin Church, had pressed the need to use and support the friendly Natives throughout the conflict, and sought to use Native tactics and skills in fighting. In June 1676 he met with the female Sachem, Awashonks, in Narragansett Bay, at a place called Treaty Rock. Awashonks agreed to join forces with the English and to hunt Philip down.

On 30 July, John Cotton was preaching in the Plymouth meeting house to a congregation which included Benjamin Church, who was resting from his intense labours. The service was interrupted by a message from Josiah Winslow that the town of Taunton was in great danger as a huge army of Natives had been seen massing on the shore of the river nearby. Church responded with his mixed company and, unknowingly, narrowly missed killing Philip as he crossed the river on a fallen tree. The following morning, Church and his men fell on the encampment where, again, they narrowly missed killing Philip who escaped into the woods. Over the next couple of days Church tracked the Sachem through the dense countryside, capturing elements of Philip's forces on the way. Although they failed to capture Philip on this occasion, Church's band of about forty men managed to take captive 173 Native prisoners.

On August 11, Church received the news he had been waiting to hear: Philip was at Mount Hope and a deserting Native was ready to lead them to him. Church gathered together his band of brothers and cautiously made his way to the swamp at the base of Mount Hope and surrounded Philip's shelter. Once the Sachem became aware of the ambush, he ran into the swamp. A Pocasset named Alderman fired the shot which effectively ended the war: Philip's body fell into the muddy waters.

The war cost the English around eight percent of its male population but the price for the

Facing page: 'Captain' Benjamin Church was among those who called for the use and support of friendly Natives in the fight against King Philip's forces

Above: Marker showing the place of King Philip's death at Mount Hope

Natives was much higher. At the start of the conflict there were about 20,000 Native People but the two–year struggle had cost them 2,000 dead, along with a further 3,000 who died of sickness and starvation and 1,000 were sent away as slaves whilst others fled further afield. A few earnest voices were heard protesting the treatment of the Natives, but the mixed multitude of settlers had little time or inclination to show mercy to any of them, especially as stories of Native savagery abounded. Many of the colonists were deeply mistrusting of the so-called converted Natives, re-naming them 'Preying Indians'. John Cotton and others lamented the lack of mercy shown to the Natives, calling the indiscriminate brutality by English soldiers: 'God's frowne upon the army'.

Salem witch trials

On 18 June 1689, the inhabitants of Salem Village appointed Samuel Parris as their minister for a stipend of £66 annually. Parris had emigrated from London in the early 1660s, attended Harvard College, and was the fourth minister appointed to Salem Village. He soon upset the fickle parishioners and they stopped paying his stipend in 1691. Parris had two servants, a female named Tituba and her husband, John. Tituba was accused by Parris' daughter, Betty, of being a witch. Betty, aged just nine, was prone to fits which were attributed to witchcraft. Her cousin, Abigail Williams aged 11, also suffered from similar convulsions and both behaved in a peculiar manner, throwing things around the house, shrieking and screaming and contorting their bodies into strange positions. The girls complained that Tituba and others were using witchcraft against them. The local doctor, William Griggs, also concluded that the fits were most likely the results of 'bewitchment'. Other young women in Salem also began to behave in a similar strange manner.

In February 1692, Tituba was arrested on suspicion of being a witch and she made a confession which implicated two others, Sarah Osborne and a homeless beggar Sarah Good, who were also arrested. Panic began to spread and further complaints were made against Dorothy Good, Martha Corey and Rebecca Nurse; Dorothy Good, aged four, was the daughter of Sarah Good

The Puritans and witchcraft

Whilst the Salem Witch trials have become legendary, the previous century saw 'Witch Trials' at their height in England. The self-styled 'Witch Finder General', Matthew Hopkins is believed to have been responsible for the deaths of some 300 women accused of witchcraft in a reign of terror from 1644–1646. Modern understanding of the Puritan's role in these events is formed through the writings of those who were largely unsympathetic towards them – presenting parody and caricature as fact. Whilst the Puritan settlers were keenly aware of the spiritual realities of evil, they were reluctant to declare witchcraft as the cause of many complaints. They were voices of caution in allegations of witchcraft and insisted on careful enquiry. Puritan William Perkins in his Way of Discovery of Witches published a series of 'Presumptions' highlighting common perceptions which fall short of proof as to whether an accused person was a witch. Cotton Mather included a number of these Presumptions in his writings and advice to the New England court before which many accused appeared. Despite the interventions of godly men, superstition, resentment and mischief exacted a terrible toll on the town of Salem.

Right: Salem Waterfront

Bottom: Samuel Parris, the unfortunate minister of Salem Village

and the others were committed members of the local church. The paranoia increased with men as well as women falling victim to accusations until 150 people were detained, awaiting trial and facing the death penalty for the capital crime of witchcraft. There are many theories about the origins of the Salem witch hysteria, but bad relationships and petty jealousies seem to have been at the root of many of the allegations.

A special court called Oyer (to hear) and Terminer (to decide), operating under English civil law, was convened under Chief Justice William Stoughton. The first

Above: Tituba and the children *by William Cullen Bryant*

to appear was Bridget Bishop, a sixty year old tavern owner, who was swiftly convicted and hanged on 10 June 1692. The court was then suspended for 20 days to take advice from some of New England's most prominent ministers, including Cotton Mather. Mather had studied cases of witchcraft reported over Europe and North America and had successfully ministered to and 'rehabilitated' four children said to have been demonized as a result

Rebecca Nurse

Nurse was born in Great Yarmouth (England) and settled in Danvers in 1640. She was a member of the Salem church and well regarded in the community. Her husband, Francis, served as Salem's Constable. It is most likely that Nurse was accused of being a witch as a result of land disputes with her accusers, the Putnam family. The community was shocked and thirty-nine prominent members signed a petition on her behalf; several testified to the court in her favour. Ann Putnam claimed that Nurse's spectre was tormenting her and broke into fits. The jury initially ruled that Nurse was not guilty but a public outcry led to a reconsideration and Nurse was hanged on 19 July 1692.

She was buried in a shallow grave but her family recovered her body and buried her in the homestead

grounds. Nurse's conviction marked a turning point in the trials. Putnam later apologized to the family for making false accusations. In 1711 the government compensated them for her wrongful death. The court of Oyer and Terminer was dismissed at the end of 1692 and the Superior Court of Judicature tried the outstanding cases. Many of those held since the middle of 1692 were tried and found not guilty or had the charges dismissed, although several were convicted but subsequently pardoned by Governor Phipps. Tituba was never tried or executed despite her confession that Satan himself had appeared to her. She was released from jail in 1693 but nothing more is known of her after that.

Above: Rebecca Nurse Homestead. Nurse was accused of witchcraft and hanged but later declared innocent

of their contact with a woman who claimed to be a witch. He spent time with them, prayed for them and helped them to recover from violent fits of temper and mysterious pains – largely as a result of their being half starved.

In his written advice to the court, Mather thanked God for disclosing the 'abominable witchcrafts' but called for caution and even tenderness towards those accused who were formerly of an unblemished character. He also called for extreme caution in the use of 'spectral evidence' – the appearance of the accuser's spirit (or ghost) to the victim – and insisted that any evidence used to convict should be of greater substance.

Sadly, the court ignored this caution and in the majority of cases, 'spectral' evidence was the undoing of the accused, nineteen of whom would hang and one, Giles Corey, was 'pressed to death'. Established in England in the 1275 Standing Mute Act and abolished in 1772, the practice of *peine forte et dure* was resorted to in the case of notorious criminals who refused to make a plea. The accused was forced to lie on his back, and weights of iron and stone were placed on the chest until they either made their plea or expired under the burden.

Thirty people accused the town's former minister, George Burroughs, of being a chief witch. Burroughs was arrested, tried and sentenced to death. At the gallows, he protested his innocence and repeated the Lord's Prayer, something considered impossible for 'witches'. The

crowd was so moved by his evident godliness that Cotton Mather felt forced to intervene and remind them that Burroughs had been properly convicted in a court of law. Increase Mather wrote a tract entitled 'Cases of conscience' in which he drew attention to the dubious and subjective nature of the evidence presented, stating that it 'were better that ten suspected witches should escape than one innocent person should be condemned.' He exhorted the court to exclude 'spectral evidence'. Governor Phipps responded by disbarring it and the lives of a further 28 accused were thereby saved.

The Deerfield Massacre

The town of Deerfield was the northernmost town of the Massachusetts settlements, exposed to attack by the French who now dominated Canada and

Above: Historic Deerfield. The scene of the 1704 massacre in which 100 people were taken captive and around 50 were killed by Natives

Below: Historic Deerfield. Showing the reproduction of the first minister's house

who sought greater control of New England whilst restricting northwards expansion of the English. The ensuing eleven year conflict came to be known as Queen Anne's War in which France and Britain fought for dominance of the continent.

In 1704 Deerfield was attacked by around 300 French and Native warriors. The town was ransacked and over 100 people were taken captive and around 50 others were killed (see also in this series *Travel with Jonathan Edwards* by Michael Haykin and Ron Baines). A young boy named Stephen Williams was captured with his family. His father, John, was the pastor of the little community and as such was a prominent target for the invaders who brutally murdered his six year old son and daughter as well as a servant. Stephen witnessed the death of his mother, who was tomahawked when she became too weak to walk, and several other women as they were led through deep snow into Canada. John did his best to help and encourage the other captives, who, in addition to the severe privations they suffered, were told to renounce their Protestantism and convert to Catholicism. John returned to Deerfield towards the end of 1706 and wrote a book about the experience, *The Redeemed captive returning to Zion*, which influenced James Fenimore Cooper in his writing of *The Last of The Mohicans'*. One of John's daughters, Eunice, never returned to Deerfield and married one of the Native People.

Despite the trauma of this

experience, Stephen Williams became a Christian minister and had considerable sympathy for the Indians. Thirty four years later, together with Nehemiah Bull from Westfield, he met with local Housatonic tribesmen to propose that a Christian mission be established among them. These Natives were some of the remnant of the once strong (20,000 member) Algonquian tribe which had been dispersed from the Hudson River in New York. The outcome of the meeting was positive and sealed with a belt of wampum as a token of the Natives' sincerity. Shortly afterwards, John Sergeant visited the Indians and was encouraged by their response to him, although he was under no illusions about the amount of work to be done. In late August 1735 a further meeting took place, involving Governor Belcher, to formalize the sending of two missionaries – John Sergeant and Timothy Woodbridge – to the Natives. One of the Native chiefs, Konkapot, told the Governor: 'We are desirous to receive the gospel of our Lord Jesus Christ and hope that our hearts are in what we say, and that we don't speak only out of our lips.'

John Sergeant

John Sergeant was born in New Jersey in 1710 to Jonathan and Mary Sergeant. The family business was farming but John had been injured and lost the use of his left hand in an accident with a scythe which turned his aim towards study, enrolling at Yale in 1725 at the age of 15. He excelled at his studies and was appointed a tutor there in 1731. Sergeant was approached, and readily agreed, to become the missionary and pastor to the Stockbridge Natives. He made arrangements to conclude his commitments at Yale and in October he met with the Natives at Skatekook (Sheffield) and Wnahktukook (Stockbridge).

Sergeants first objective was to erect a building which would serve as school and meetinghouse at a suitable point between the two settlements. He completed his academic year at Yale and

Right: A 1900 depiction of the raid on Deerfield (Walter Henry Lippincott)

took with him two sons of Chiefs Konkapot and Umpachane who studied English during the day and taught Sergeant their own languages in the evening. In 1735 John returned to the villages and within a few months around forty Natives had professed faith in Christ and were baptized. Sergeant continued his studies into the Native language and translated several portions of Scripture, prayers and a catechism. In 1736 the Massachusetts General Court granted the formation of a township between the two settlements and although it was originally called 'Indian Town' it later became known as Stockbridge. Isaac Hollis – a London minister – provided support for twelve Native boys to remain at the school and be taught. Timothy Woodbridge of Springfield (whose mother was John Eliot's granddaughter) took the position as schoolmaster and four English families were allowed to settle in the new town with a view to providing the Natives models of civilized behaviour.

Sergeant's ministry among the Natives at Stockbridge saw around 130 (about half of the Native population) baptized before his death. The English contingent grew to ten families, and among the fifty or so residences which sprang up along the main street, some twenty were English in style. Sergeant died in the summer of 1749 at only 39 years of age. Timothy Woodbridge oversaw the mission for the next two years while Stockbridge was without

Below: Stockbridge Mission House. The home of John Sergeant the 'Apostle to the Indians'

a resident minister until the Rev. Jonathan Edwards who had been forced from his ministry at Northampton was appointed in Sergeant's place. In 1751 Edwards moved to Stockbridge from where he served as missionary to 150 Mohawk and Mohegan families at a time of real tensions between the English and the French who often conducted raids into the Connecticut Valley. The site of the house he occupied is marked by a small marble fountain and there is a memorial to him on the green. (See in this series *Travel with Jonathan Edwards* by Michael Haykin and Ron Baines).

Above: David Brainerd preaching to the Natives

Sergeant was held in a high degree of honour by the Natives who mourned the loss of their minister who they believed always dealt with them fairly. They would, in turn, respond to the call to help the English against the French and Native assaults from Canada. They would also be one of only two tribes to support the colonists against the British in the war of Independence. In 1775, the mission was taken up by his son John Sergeant Jnr. but sadly, perceived injustices over land deals perpetrated by the white population gradually forced the Natives to abandon the town.

David Brainerd

In the spring of 1743, David Brainerd rode to Stockbridge to meet John Sergeant. Brainerd had been appointed as a missionary to the Natives in Pennsylvania by the Scottish Society for the Propagation of Christian Knowledge which had become concerned with the need for evangelism in the new colonies. After just one night, he rode on to Kaunaumeek where he spent his first night on the mission field. On Sunday 10 April 1743 Brainerd preached to the Natives and found them to be generally amenable to his message, having previously come into contact with John Sergeant. One or two expressed concern for their spiritual state. He stayed about a year but did not always find the work so encouraging. Brainerd built a ' house' to live in because he had been 'sleeping rough' in conditions which were far from helpful to his poor health. He describes his lodgings as 'a heap of straw, laid on some boards, a little way from the floor; for it is a log room without any floor, that I lodge in'. He also secured the services of an Indian interpreter named John Wauwaumpequunaunt who had served with John Sergeant. Brainerd made regular visits to Sergeant at Stockbridge and they

Above: *A Native in a meeting house (Plimoth Plantation)*

worked together on the Native language and customs, seeking ways to reach them with the gospel of Jesus. In May of 1744 he moved on to Pennsylvania but it was at Kaunaumeek that he learned the rudiments of ministry to the Natives which would prove to be so valuable at the Forks of the Delaware and Crossweeksung (now Crosswicks New Jersey) where he was to experience such blessing among the Natives.

Brainerd made a few trips back to New England during the coming years. In May 1747, with his health rapidly deteriorating, he made his final journey to Northampton, to the home of his friend Jonathan Edwards. His intention was to recuperate and to 'recover his health by riding' as he had been prescribed by others to do, but it would mark the close of his ministry among the Natives and draw down the veil on his earthly existence. A doctor was called to the home where David's tuberculosis was diagnosed ('consumption' as it was then known): there was no hope of recovery.

Once again, the prescription was to ride and so he rode the three days journey to Boston, accompanied by Edwards' daughter Jerusha who had already become something of a soulmate for David and a pillar of support for him during the closing days of his life. In Boston they stayed at the home of Joseph Bromfield where David became gravely ill. Remarkably, he recovered sufficiently to make the return journey to Edwards' home in Northampton, arriving on 25 July. Here he spent quiet days in the pleasant company of Edwards and his wife Sarah, but by September he was unable to leave his room and Jerusha faithfully ministered to him as the illness consumed his body. On the morning of the 9 October 1747 he passed into the presence of the Lord he had so earnestly and faithfully served and proclaimed. The funeral service was held in the Northampton church and David was buried in the cemetery at

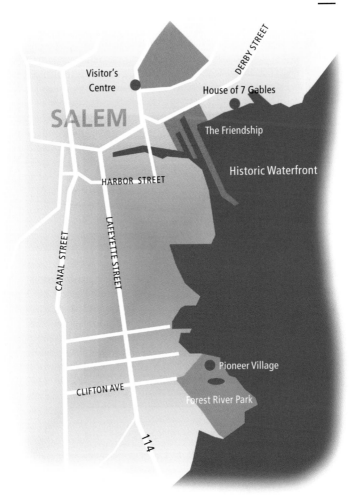

Above: Map of Salem – showing historic waterfront and Pioneer Village

Bridge Street.

TRAVEL INFORMATION

Salem

Salem is obsessed with the ghoulish horrors of the Witch Trials which bear its name, and many of the so–called attractions of the town focus on this dark period of history. Despite this, however, Salem has a few gems which should not be missed. The historic docklands, from which Adoniram Judson and friends sailed to Burma, and Pioneer Village – a faithful recreation of huts and houses built by the first settlers are in themselves sufficient to redeem the town. The Witch Trials are nevertheless significant events which throw light on the development of

Christian understanding and thinking in the early 17th century. An unfortunate statue of Roger Conant, looking like a cloaked wizard, stands in front of the Witch Museum in Salem.

House of the Seven Gables

At one time owned by a cousin of the author Nathaniel Hawthorne, the House of the Seven Gables was originally built in 1675 for Captain John Turner. It has undergone numerous extensions and alterations over a period of 100 years. The house is now a museum and Hawthorne's birthplace has been moved from its original location onto the same site at Union Street.

Website: 7gables.org
Historic waterfront

In the information centre of Salem historic waterfront is a plaque commemorating the departure of the first international missionaries from the United States: Adoniram Judson, Samuel Newell, Samuel Nott, Gordon Hall and Luther Rice. Judson and his friends set out from this harbour to Burma aboard the Caravan in 1812. Visitors are able to walk around several historic houses and maritime exhibits as well as visit the replica of the Friendship, a reconstruction of a 1797 East Indiaman, a merchant ship operating under charter to the English East India Company, of a kind similiar to the one in which Judson sailed.

Website: nps.gov/sama

First Church

On the 6 February 1812 in Salem Tabernacle, the oldest Protestant Church in America, almost 2,000 people attended a commissioning service for Adoniram Judson, Samuel Newell, Samuel Nott, Gordon Hall and Luther Rice. The present (1924) church at 50 Washington Street still has the bench on which the men and their wives sat, and boasts of owning a cello played at the service. The First Baptist Church of Salem at 292 Lafayette Street has a stained glass window depicting the ship *Caravan*, on which Adoniram departed from the harbour nearby on 19 February.

Rebecca Nurse Homestead

Located at 149 Pine Street, Danvers, Salem, this house was built around 1678 and was inhabited by Rebecca Nurse who was accused of witchcraft and hanged in 1692 at the age of 71. The house is now a museum which contains period artefacts and there are other buildings on the grounds including a reconstruction of the earliest Salem meetinghouse.

Website: rebeccanurse.org

Historic Deerfield

Today the town is known as Historic

Above: The House of the Seven Gables – Nathaniel Hawthorne based his famous 1851 novel on the house and its history, examining New England life in the shadow of the Salem Witch Trials

Deerfield and is a living history museum comprised of many 18th century houses, several of which are open to the public, including the Ashley House, home of the Rev. Jonathan Ashley, minister to the town. A guided visit to this house is worthwhile to hear of the difficulties between the town and their rather ambitious minister.

Website: historic–deerfield.org/

Stockbridge Mission House

In 1739, John Sergeant built his own house in the settlement and this can still be visited on Main Street in modern Stockbridge. Originally standing on Prospect Hill, the building was dismantled and reassembled on Main Street in the late 1920's under the direction of Miss Mabel Choate who was then the owner of the nearby historic estate at Naumkeag. The house contains a collection of 18th century American furniture and there is a small museum of Mohican exhibits. The town also hosts the Norman Rockwell Museum which holds one of the artists' paintings of John Sergeant and Chief Konkapot. A stone memorial marks the spot where the first meeting house once stood.

Website: search for The Mission House, Stockbridge.

Northampton

Bridge Street Cemetery
A stone marks David Brainerds' grave. Visitors to the church and cemetery will also notice nearby the headstone of a grave marking the death of Jerusha Edwards who followed him to glory only a few months later, at the age of 18 years. Although Jonathan Edwards is buried elsewhere there is also a stone commemorating his life and ministry in the same section of the cemetery.

Top: *Salem Historic Waterfront*

Above: *The Friendship – a replica 1797 East Indiaman of a type familiar to Adoniram Judson in which he sailed to Burma as a missionary in 1812*

⑧ The winds of change

Boston's priority over Plymouth continued to increase, as well as its success in planting communities in the Massachusetts area

I n 1643 an Article of Confederation was signed in which the colonies of Massachusetts, Plymouth, Connecticut and New Haven pledged themselves to a league of friendship and cooperation for the 'preserving and propagating the Gospel' and for their mutual safety and benefit. Each of the colonies sent two delegates and agreed to provide a number of soldiers for the common cause. The plantation at Plymouth struggled to compete with the power of its neighbour and gradually fell into decline.

In the mid 1600's the founding fathers, Brewster, Winslow, Bradford and others who had been pillars of the fledgling community died; including 'Captain' Standish who had never joined the church at Plymouth. Even the Leiden church in Holland closed in 1655, struggling to pay its bills in the wake of the 1620 exodus; the loss of their beloved Pastor Robinson was too much for it to bear.

Above: Kings Chapel, Boston, erected in 1749 around an old wooden meeting house that was then dismantled and passed out through the windows of the new building

Facing page: 'Bostonians paying the excise man – tarring and feathering the tax collector' (1774 British print by Philip Dawe)

All the King's Men
In 1680, Charles II decided to take further control of New England's colonies and called for reforms of

Cotton Mather and the inoculation controversy

From 1677 to 1702, there were three major outbreaks of smallpox in the colony that proved devastating to both Natives and settlers. In 1721 HMS Seahorse arrived from the West Indies and brought a further epidemic of the disease. By September, the death toll had reached over 100 and all attempts to stem the tide by quarantine had failed. Cotton Mather was the grandson of Richard Mather and John Cotton on his mother's side. He graduated from Harvard at the age of fifteen and shortly afterwards joined his father in ministry at Boston's original North Church in North Square, becoming its sole minister in 1685. He was a powerful character and prolific writer who acquired considerable influence in both the secular and spiritual government of the colony. Mather

had heard from a slave, many years before, of the practice of inoculation and wrote to local doctors urging them to consider it in the present dilemma.

Only Dr Zabdiel Boylston was persuaded to attempt the procedure, first on his own household and then on over 240 people, of whom only six died. However, both Boylston and Mather were vilified and threatened for their part in this strange practice. On one occasion a hand grenade was thrown into Boylston's home but it failed to explode. The issue caused division amongst the Puritans who struggled to understand how causing injury (by inoculation) was consistent with the Biblical principle of healing. Boylston later pioneered other medical techniques including mastectomy and the removal of gall bladder stones.

Above: Cotton Mather – Puritan minister who became embroiled in the Salem Witch Trials and was vilified for his support of inoculation against smallpox

the Massachusetts Bay Colony – which they disregarded. Four years later Charles revoked its charter but died before further action could be taken. When James II succeeded to the throne he continued the process of bringing the colonies under tighter control of the Crown and appointed Sir Edmund Andros as Governor of New England.

Andros' rule was autocratic and hugely unpopular.

On his arrival in Boston as Governor of New England in December 1686, Andros asked the Puritan churches if services of the Church of England might be held in their premises temporarily. He was summarily rebuffed and so acquired a plot of land on the town burial ground in Tremont Street. A wooden chapel – King's Chapel – was built for the use of the king's men who enforced British law. When this became too small, the present building was erected around it and the old one dismantled and passed out through the windows. In this way services of worship continued for the five year period whilst the new chapel was being constructed. In 1784 Rev. James Freeman began teaching Unitarian doctrine here, revising the prayer book to accord with those doctrines. Unitarianism opposes the mainstream Christian doctrine concerning the Trinity, teaching instead that Jesus was not God but a great man or possibly even a supernatural being. Followers also teach that rational thought, science and philosophy are on a level with the teachings of Jesus and that human nature is not inherently sinful. Unitarianism began to spread across the Congregational churches of New England and the visitor will find that many of the pioneering works of the 17th century have now succumbed to its teachings.

The Old South Meeting House was built in 1729 and its first pastor was Thomas Thatcher from Salisbury, England. The congregation was a split from John Winthrop's own First Church Congregation in 1669. Being the largest building in the area, it soon became used as a place for public meetings, often in protest against British taxes and policies.

On 12 October 1740 the evangelist visiting from England, George Whitefield, preached at Old South but the place was so full that he was obliged to climb in thorough one of the windows. This service was followed by one on the common where it is estimated 20,000 people attended. Whitefield's reflections on the city of Boston are recorded in his journals: 'Boston is a large, populous place, and very wealthy. It has the form of religion kept up, but has lost much of its power.' His insight echoes powerfully with Boston of the present day.

Whitefield also preached in the New South Church at Summer Street in September 1740, the minister there being Samuel Checkley. The meeting house was full to capacity, so one member of the congregation broke a board to make a seat

Above: *Old South Meeting House . Originally a Puritan meeting-house but because of its capacity was used for public meetings and became a focal point for debate and dissent*

Left: Old South Meeting House pulpit from which George Whitfield preached

Right: Phillis Wheatley poems – the first publication of an African-American woman

for himself. The sudden noise of breaking timber caused a panic to break out in which people were trampled whilst trying to escape and several threw themselves out of windows. Five people were killed and many others seriously wounded. Whitefield arrived as the events were unfolding and was greatly distressed by the incident. He announced, however, that he would preach on the common and, despite everything, several thousand followed to hear his message.

Old South exhibits a collection of poems by Phillis Wheatley. Wheatley was an 8 year old slave brought to Boston from West Africa in 1761 on a ship from which her first name is taken. She was sold to a wealthy Boston merchant, John Wheatley, from whom she takes her surname. In an unprecedented move, she was educated by the family's daughter and by the age of 12 could read Greek and Latin as well as passages from the Scriptures. She wrote poetry and became the first African–American woman to be

published. Phillis attended Old South Church and wrote a poem marking George Whitfield's death in 1770 entitled 'An Elegiac Poem, on the Death of that Celebrated Divine, and Eminent Servant of Jesus Christ, the Reverend and Learned George Whitefield' which contained the following lines:

HAIL, happy saint, on thine immortal throne,
Possest of glory, life, and bliss unknown;
We hear no more the music of thy tongue,
Thy wonted auditories cease to throng.
Thy sermons in unequall'd accents flow'd,
And ev'ry bosom with devotion glow'd;
Thou didst in strains of eloquence refin'd
Inflame the heart, and captivate the mind.
Unhappy we the setting sun deplore,
So glorious once, but ah! it shines no more.

The parting of the ways

Tensions between the now thirteen well-established colonies along the Eastern shores of America and the mother country simmered and increased to boiling point in the mid 1700s. The British had defeated the French in the Seven Years War but were in need of raising finances to pay for the conflict. For the first time, the British Parliament began to impose direct taxation on the colonies. The Sugar Tax which imposed duty on goods brought into New England and restricted the export of certain goods only to England, and the Stamp Act which imposed duty on various kinds of printing material were fuel to the fire of American indignation. Samuel Adams, a Harvard trained politician and son of a Puritan family, headed up the opposition on the basis that the Colonies were not represented in Parliament – giving rise to the battle cry: 'No taxation without representation'. Boston became the centre of organised resistance against the British interference, and four British Army regiments were sent to keep order. Skirmishes between the army and the Bostonians took place over the coming months and hostility grew.

Following the 'Boston Massacre' of 1770 when nervous British soldiers fired on a crowd and killed five people, Old South was used to hold a meeting of several thousand outraged Bostonians. Two years later, almost 5,000 people crowded into the meeting house to debate the infamous Tea Tax. Samuel Adams used the meetings to good advantage and orchestrated the events which led to what became known as 'The Boston Tea Party'. With the arrival of the three shipments of British East India Company tea to Boston, the tax on tea, implemented by the passing of the 1767 Townshend Revenue Act, had to be paid the moment the tea was unloaded from the *Beaver*, *Dartmouth*, and *Eleanor*. If the tax was not paid within the twenty days following

Below: The Old State House, Boston, in front of which the 'Boston Massacre' of 1770 took place

Bottom: Marker showing the site of the 'Boston Massacre'

the ships' arrival, the ships and their cargoes of tea would be seized by the authorities.

The Boston Tea Party

On the night of Thursday 16 December, 1773, members of the 'Sons of Liberty' disguised as Mohawk Indians and armed with axes, boarded the three ships moored at Griffin's Wharf. In a span of three hours, 340 chests – over 92,000 pounds – of British East India Company tea were smashed and dumped into Boston Harbour.

The implications and impact of the Boston Tea Party were enormous. On hearing of the events, the British Parliament was appalled and instituted a series of enactments stripping Massachusetts of her independence and right of self governance. Lord North, the Prime Minister of England declared, 'The Americans have tarred and feathered your subjects, plundered your merchants, burnt your ships, denied all obedience to your laws and authority; yet so clement and so long forbearing has our conduct been that it is incumbent on us now to take a different course. Whatever may be the consequences, we must risk something; if we do not, all is over.'

These acts became known in New England as the Intolerable Acts – or Coercive Acts – and embittered the Americans further in their dispute with the homeland. The American Revolution on 19 April 1775 can, in part, be traced directly to the events which took place in Boston Harbour in 1773. When war between the British and Americans finally broke out in 1775, the British took over the Old South Meeting House and deliberately vandalized the church, filling it with gravel and

using it to house their animals as well as their troops. It was several years before the congregation could afford the funds to repair the church in which they continued to worship until 1876 when they relocated into Copley Square. The meeting house was auctioned and saved for the nation as a museum. The bitter war of independence came to its close in 1783 with the signing of the Treaty of Paris. King George III conceded the land to the settlers and withdrew.

The first colonists had earnestly sought to remain faithful to the king, even whilst escaping his influence in matters of faith, but now New England issued divorce papers to the wife of their youth. In just over 150 years, the heroic efforts and high ideals of the first settlers had largely evaporated. They founded a New World but it did not enshrine the spiritual ideals they so cherished – and they had brought the seeds of their own destruction with them. They discovered what Noah and his sons discovered after the flood, that sin cannot be eradicated by 'natural' efforts alone or 'left behind' in an old country.

Visitors to New England today will perhaps be surprised to discover how many churches established by these pioneers and their well-known descendants have fallen to Unitarianism or have in some other way abandoned Bible truth altogether. Even the revivals seen in the subsequent days of Edwards, Nettleton, Whitefield and many others are just a distant memory. Boston today is a delightful, charming and friendly city to visit but is so far from Winthrop's vision of a 'City on a hill' that it seems to champion everything the Puritans stood against.

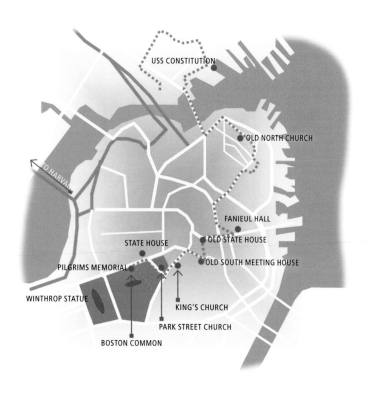

Above: Map of historic sites in Boston, showing the Freedom Trail

TRAVEL INFORMATION

Freedom Trail

The Freedom Trail is a 2.5 mile trail marked in red on central Boston's footpaths and leads visitors on a tour of 16 of the most important sites in Boston's colourful history. Sites relevant to this book are listed below. Other sites of interest are not far from the trail and are detailed towards the end of the list. Website: freedomtrail.org

Boston Common

George Whitefield preached here in September 1740 to an estimated crowd of over 15,000 people. On the northern boundary of the common is the Founders Memorial and on the reverse in Beacon Street is a quote from Winthrop's 'City on a hill' speech. Some of the most severe punishments for infringements of the colony's strict rules were carried out here and several people were hanged from the Great Elm Tree (now marked only by a plaque).

Massachusetts State House

At the northern end of Boston Common, the 'New' State House was opened in 1798 and stands on land originally used by John Hancock to pasture his cows. The striking golden dome was gilded with 23 carat gold for the first time in 1874 but painted black in World War II to protect the city from airborne attack. As well as statues of Mary Dyer and Anne Hutchinson, which can only be viewed from the road outside, visitors can tour the State House with a guide at no cost. Website: cityofboston.gov

Park Street Church

Park Street church stands opposite Boston Common and has an imposing spire which is 66m high. The building was completed in a single year and worship services commenced in 1810. In 1819 the church was the first to send missionaries to the Hawaiian islands. Park Street hosted an evangelistic campaign by C G Finney in 1858, and a crusade by Billy Graham in 1949. As the congregation at Old South Church drifted towards Unitarianism, a number wanted to establish an orthodox church in Boston's centre. Despite opposition, 26 people, mostly former members

of the Old South, formed a 'Religious Improvement Society' in 1804. They met together for prayer and Biblical instruction and five years later founded Park Street Church. The 1809 Covenant includes the words: 'We hereby covenant and engage ... to give up ourselves unto the Lord ... to unite together into one body for the public worship of God, and the mutual edification one of another in the fellowship of the Lord Jesus: exhorting, reproving, comforting and watching over each other, for mutual edification; looking for that blessed hope and the glorious appearing of ... our Saviour JESUS ....'

Park Street became known as 'Brimstone Corner' – partly because of its uncompromising gospel preaching and partly because the basement was used as a gunpowder store in the 1812 conflict between the United States and Great Britain. Park Street also took a lead role in the anti–slavery movement, hosting a series of lectures from 1823 onwards. In Massachusetts, slaves had been free since 1781, but the debate continued to threaten the wider union of the states. Massachusetts was the first state to end the ban on interracial marriage (1843), the first to desegregate public schools (1855), the first to admit black jurors (1860), and the first northern state to raise a black regiment during the Civil War.
Website: parkstreet.org

King's Chapel and burying ground

The burying ground adjacent to the chapel contains the Winthrop family tomb and that of Mary Chilton – the first woman reported to have stepped off the Mayflower. The Cotton family tomb is here as well as that of Puritan John Davenport.
Website: kings-chapel.org

Above: Park Street Church

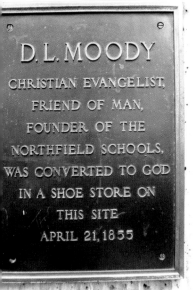

D. L. MOODY

CHRISTIAN EVANGELIST,
FRIEND OF MAN,
FOUNDER OF THE
NORTHFIELD SCHOOLS,
WAS CONVERTED TO GOD
IN A SHOE STORE ON
THIS SITE
APRIL 21, 1855

Top: *The Winthrop tomb at King's Chapel burying ground*

Above: *D L Moody Plaque, Court Street, Boston*

Old South Meeting House

The original 1669 Puritan Meeting House was a wooden structure which was replaced by the present building in 1729. Its large capacity meant that it was often used for public meetings, debate and protest.
Website: oldsouthmeetinghouse.org

Old State House

In the centre of the city, dwarfed by the surrounding modern office blocks, stands the 300 year old State House situated at the junction of Washington and State Streets. This was the seat of government between 1713 and 1798. A plaque on the street outside marks the place where, in 1770, an altercation between British soldiers and a crowd of Bostonians escalated into what is now known as the Boston Massacre. Five Bostonians died and the city was galvanized in its resistance to British rule without representation.

Website: revolutionaryboston.org/
Nearby is a plaque commemorating the conversion of D L Moody.

At 17 years of age, Moody went to Boston to work in his uncle's shoe store in Court Street. He began to attend Mount Vernon Congregational Church and was placed in the Sunday school class of Edward D Kimball. Kimball's practice was to visit his students during the week and he sought Moody out at the shoe store and told him of Christ's love. Today a plaque marks the location of the store and the moment of Moody's conversion in the back room.

Old North Church (Christ Church)

Situated in Boston's North End, the Old North Church built in 1723 was founded by the Rev. Timothy Cutler, a graduate

Above: Old North Church pulpit

Below: Wesley plaque in Old North Church

of Harvard and one–time rector of Yale College in New Haven. In 1722, on what became known as the 'Dark Day at Yale', Cutler and six other Congregational ministers declared their allegiance to the Anglican church – something that 'burst like a terrible bombshell in the heart of the New England camp.' Despite its strong ties to the English crown, the church is most famous for its role in the American Revolution when its tower was used to show lanterns to warn of the impending British assault in 1775.

It is the oldest church in Boston and visitors can see the closed pews and lofty pulpit from which Charles Wesley preached in 1736. Wesley was just a young novice minister returning to the UK from Georgia but the ship was diverted to Boston for repairs. Wesley stayed for just over a month during which time he also preached at King's Chapel. He is known to have preached a sermon written by his brother, John, on Luke 10:42 entitled 'The one thing needful'. Wesley was ill throughout his time in Boston and could not be dissuaded from boarding his ship for home at the earliest opportunity. The Mather family tomb stands in Copps Hill burying ground, near to the Old North Church.

Website: oldnorth.com

The following sites of interest are not on the Freedom Trail:

Boston Public Library

A statue of Henry Vane stands in the entrance lobby of the library in Boston's Copley Square. Vane arrived in the colony from England in 1635 on the Abigail. He lived with John Cotton and

---

The Rev. Charles Wesley. M.A. (1707-1788)

Co-founder of Methodism preached in this church in September and October 173

Sweet singer of evangelical Anglicanism and poet of jubilant Methodis

† † †

PRESENTED BY THE COUNCIL OF BISHOPS OF THE METHODIST CHURCH
SEPTEMBER 24, 1961

joined Anne Hutchinson's Bible studies which had grown to around eighty people by that time. Vane was in favour of religious tolerance and continued to support her. When recalled to England, Vane became a significant member of Parliament under Oliver Cromwell's patronage until that relationship also soured. Vane opposed Cromwell's plans for a new government and when Cromwell dissolved Parliament, it was he who protested that the actions were 'against morality and decency'. Vane eventually was hanged in 1662 on Tower Hill for high treason against the king. The library is well worth a visit not only for the statue, but also for its impressive and extravagant interior design. Visitors will also appreciate the quiet, cool courtyard in the centre of the complex, as well as the ornate staircase and grand reading room

Website: bpl.org

John Winthrop statue

(see page 60)

At the junction of Marlborough Street and Exeter Street in Back Bay is a statue of John Winthrop by Richard Saltonstall Greenough. This work is a bronze replica of a marble statue of Winthrop in the U S Capitol building, Washington DC. Its present location at the side of First Church Boston is the last in a series of moves necessitated by development work in Boston Centre. In 1968 a fire seriously damaged First Church and Winthrop's statue was decapitated. Although the pieces were initially recovered, the head was subsequently lost and had to be re–cast. In 1975 the statue was returned to its location at the side of the renovated First Church. Visitors to Boston's Winthrop Square on Devonshire Street will be surprised to find that the statue there is in fact Robert Burns the poet!

Top: *Henry Vane, Governor of the Massachusetts Bay Colony from 1636–1637. By Frederick William MacMonnies (1863–1937). Boston Public Library*

Above: *John Winthrop statue*

The developers of the square approached First Church with a request for Winthrop to stand in the square that bears his name but this was declined and they had to make do with Burns whose statue languished in the Boston Fens until being given a new home in Winthrop Square.

Trinity Church

Founded in 1733, Trinity Church originally stood in Summer Street but was destroyed by the great fire of 1872. The rector, Philips Brooks – most well-known for his hymn 'O Little Town of Bethlehem'– supervised the erection of the new building which still stands in Copley Square. As the square was built on reclaimed marsh land, Trinity stands on over 4500 wooden piles driven into the wet ground. It is ornately decorated with over 21000 square feet of murals as well as many impressive stained glass windows including several designed by the English textile designer, William Morris. The church has been designated as one of the ten most significant buildings in all the United States. It now stands in the shadow of the John Hancock Tower which acts as a mirror enhancing the views of the church. Website: trinitychurchboston.org/

Congregational House and Library

14 Beacon Street
The Congregational House and library

Below: Trinity Church – Boston

Above: Memorial to Philips Brooks, minister of Trinity Church and author of 'O Little Town of Bethlehem'

hosts almost a quarter of a million documents tracing the development of Congregationalism in the United States. The building is decorated with several bas reliefs depicting the colonists at Shawmut Peninsula, signing the covenant to form First Church, Henry Vane proposing the formation of a school to educate ministers and John Eliot preaching to the Natives.

African Meeting House

The meetinghouse was built in 1806 and is the oldest known existing black church in the United States. Even though it was built to house an African congregation, at its opening, the floor level seats in the centre were reserved for those 'benevolently disposed to the Africans' whilst black members were restricted to the balcony. The meetinghouse is open to the public for tours.
Website: afroammuseum.org

Museum of Fine Arts

The museum has some excellent exhibits and is well worth time to visit when in Boston if at all possible. Some of the Egyptian exhibits complement Biblical artefacts found in the British Museum – including the sarcophagus of Queen Hatshepsut, daughter of Thutmose 1 and a possible candidate for the woman who lifted Moses from the Nile.
Website: mfa.org

John Endecott Memorial (see page 59) An imposing white granite statue of Governor John Endecott stands at the north-east corner of the Museum of Fine Arts at Fenway. Endecott's figure was designed by Ralph Weld Gray and carved from a 12 ton block of granite by Carl Paul Jennewein. George Augustus Peabody, one of Endecott's direct descendents, made a gift of the statue to the city.

USS Constitution

Otherwise known as Old Ironsides, the name derived from the 1812 war when British Cannonballs bounced off its oak hull. Constitution is the oldest commissioned naval vessel afloat. Berthed at Pier 1 of the former Charlestown Navy Yard, at one end of Boston's Freedom Trail, serving Navy officers give guided tours in period costumes.
Website: ussconstitutionmuseum.org

Bunker Hill, Charlestown

The monument, was erected to commemorate the Battle of Bunker Hill, the first major conflict between British and Patriot forces in the American Revolutionary War, fought there on 17 June 1775. The monument is actually situated on Breeds Hill where most of the fighting took place.

Left: *The Boston Tea Party Museum*

Tea Party Ships Museum

(See page 113)

Located at Congress Street Bridge, the Tea Party Ships Museum includes live action, audience participation and multimedia displays to recreate the events of the famous Boston Tea Party.
Website: bostonteapartyship.com/

Isabella Stewart Gardner Museum

Once the elaborate home of Isabella Stewart Gardner, now a museum filled with 2,500 exhibits of art and culture from Europe and America. The museum owns works by Rembrandt, Botticelli, Raphael and Giotto as well as Degas, Matisse and Manet. Gardner's will prevents any alteration to the premises or the layout of its exhibits and so it is exactly as she left it – with the exception of a number of exhibits stolen in a 1990 robbery when two men dressed as detectives, wearing false moustaches, tricked their way into the building and stole thirteen items worth around £300 million.
Website: gardnermuseum.org/

Faneuil Hall and Quincy Market

Faneuil Hall is located near the waterfront and today's Government Centre in Boston, Massachusetts; it, has been a marketplace and a meeting hall since 1742. This was the site of several speeches by Samuel Adams, James Otis, and others encouraging independence from Great Britain. It is now part of Boston National Historical Park and a well-known stop on the Freedom Trail. Sometimes it is referred to as 'The Cradle of Liberty'.

The adjacent Quincy Market hosts a wide variety of food stalls catering for every taste.

Above: *John Adam's birthplace, Quincy*

John Adams Birthplace

Quincy (South Greater Boston)

Quincy was settled in 1625 but taken over soon after by Thomas Morton. Morton rebelled against the strict codes of conduct at Plymouth and renamed it Ma-re-mount (Hill by the sea) but intended no doubt to annoy the Puritans by its resemblance to 'Merry-Mount'. The town was regarded as a 'school of atheism' and the den of 'all (sorts of) profaneness'. In 1627 Morton was arrested by Captain Standish for conduct harmful to the colony (including the sale of guns to the Natives). He was sent back to England only to be brought back a year later by an unwitting Isaac Allerton. Quincy is the home of Adams National Historical Park. Visitors may tour the birthplace of the United State's second President, John Adams, and also the birthplace of John Quincy Adams, his son and the sixth President of the United States.

The Adams home at Peacefield is also part of the park and a trolleybus service shuttles visitors between the two main sites.
Website: nps.gov/adam

PILGRIM FATHERS' STORY

1590	Ancient Brethren (dissenting congregation) established in Amsterdam
1603	James I takes throne of England
1604	Hampton Court Conference results in preparation of King James Bible
1604	Richard Clyfton becomes Pastor of dissenting congregation at Gainsborough
1607	First attempt of Separatists to leave UK shores – betrayed by ships Master
1608	Second attempt fails – Individual families leave for Amsterdam
1609	John Robinson and congregation leave Amsterdam for Leiden
1619	Robert Cushman and John Carver agree with Virginia Company to settle in Virginia
1620	(June) *Mayflower* and *Speedwell* chartered
	(July) *Speedwell* leaves Delft Haven for rendezvous in UK
	5 August *Speedwell* and *Mayflower* set sail from Southampton
	Speedwell develops leak – ships put in to Dartmouth, two weeks for repairs
	(August) *Speedwell* and *Mayflower* depart Dartmouth
	After 300 miles *Speedwell* becomes unsafe, ships head back to Plymouth
	6 September *Mayflower* with 102 passengers and 30+ crew sets out alone
	11 November First landing at Provincetown
	11 December *Mayflower* relocates to Plymouth
	25 December Construction of first house at Plymouth begins
1621	(March) Samoset and Squanto begin to mediate with the Natives for the Pilgrims
	(April) Governor Carver dies
	(October) The first 'Thanksgiving' takes place
	(November) The *Fortune* arrives at Plymouth

Recommended Reading:

Not all books written about the Pilgrim Fathers are sympathetic to the visionary men and women who struggled to establish the New World, but they can still be read with profit. The following books are the most accessible:

Mayflower - A Story of Courage, Community and War. Nathaniel Philbrick. Penguin (2006)

Between Two Worlds: How the English Became Americans. Malcolm Gaskill. Oxford University Press (2014).

Saints and Strangers. George F. Willison. Heinemann London (1945)

Of Plymouth Plantation. William Bradford. Modern Library (1981)

Big Chief Elizabeth. Giles Milton. Hodder & Stoughton (2000)

1622	(May) Thomas Weston attempts to settle Weymouth (Wessagusset) as separate colony
1623	Supply ship *Anne* arrives with further settlers from Leiden
	(Spring) Weymouth colony collapses
1626	Salem founded by Roger Conant
1630	(April) John Winthrop's fleet sails for New England and lands at Salem
1630	1 August Settlers move to 'Trimountain' (later to be re-named 'Boston')
1635	Nineteen ships arrive at Boston
1636	College at Newtowne founded (renamed Harvard in 1639)
1643	Massachusetts, Plymouth, Connecticut and New Haven sign Article of Confederation
1675	'King Philip's War' begins
1676	(August) King Philip killed – war draws to an end
1684	Charles II revokes Massachusetts Bay Colony charter
1692	Salem Witch Trials
1704	Deerfield massacre carried out by French and Native allies
1743	Ministry of David Brainerd
1747	Brainerd dies at home of Jonathan Edwards
1770	'Boston Massacre'
1773	'Boston Tea Party' revolt against taxes imposed by Britain
1775	War of Independence between Britain and the colonies
1783	King George III concedes the land to the settlers

Note that early dates may vary by as much as ten days because of the transition between the Julian and the Gregorian calendars which took place in September 1752

About the Author

Ian Cooper is the Pastor of Tollgate Evangelical Church in Redhill, Sussex, UK where he has ministered for 20 years. He was formerly a Police Sergeant in the Wiltshire Constabulary. He is married to Jacky and they have two married daughters. Ian is a member of the Day One Council and conducts tours of the Biblical artefacts in the British Museum.

Other titles in this great series

John Bunyan
Exploring the world of John Bunyan, author of The Pilgrim's Progress

John Pestell

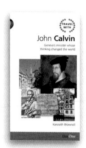

William Booth
Founder and first General of The Salvation Army

Jim Winter

John Calvin
Geneva's minister whose thinking changed the world

Kenneth Brownell

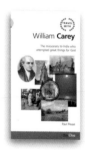

William Carey
The missionary to India who attempted great things for God

Paul Pease

William Tyndale
England's greatest bible translator

Brian H Edwards

CH Spurgeon
In the footsteps of the 'Prince of Preachers'

Clive Anderson

Jordan
Land of temples, fortresses and mosaics

Edward Dawson

John Blanchard
Guernsey's evangelist, author and Christian apologist

Brian H Edwards

Robert Murray McCheyne
In the footsteps of a godly Scottish pastor

Derek Prime

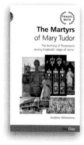

The Martyrs of Mary Tudor
The burning of Protestants during England's 'reign of terror'

Andrew Atherstone

Oxford
City of saints, scholars and dreaming spires

Andrew Atherstone

Egypt
Land of Moses, monuments and mummies

Clive and Amanda Anderson

TO ACCOMPANY THIS SERIES

▷ FOOTSTEPS OF THE PAST

John Bunyan, William Booth,
William Carey, William Wilberforce
CS Lewis, William Tyndale,
The British Museum

'…as good a compact guidebook as you are likely to find…'

A READER'S FEEDBACK ON TRAVEL THROUGH ROME

William **Cowper**
The evangelical poet

Paul Williams

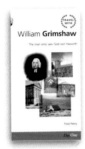

William **Grimshaw**
The man who saw God visit Haworth

Faith Cook

Frances Ridley **Havergal**
The English hymn writer and poet

Carol Purves

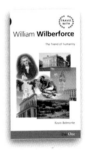

William **Wilberforce**
The friend of humanity

Kevin Belmonte

John **Knox**
In the footsteps of Scotland's great reformer

David Campbell

Billy **Graham**
In the footsteps of God's Ambassador

Kevin Belmonte

Martyn **Lloyd-Jones**
In the footsteps of the distinguished Welsh evangelist, pastor and theologian

Philip H Eveson

CS **Lewis**
The creator of Narnia and the most quoted Christian of the 20th Century

Ronald W Bresland

Cambridge
City of beauty, reformation and pioneering research

David Bewley

The Houses of **Parliament**
Cradle of democracy

Andrew Atherstone

Israel
Land of promise, faith and beauty

Paul Williams and Clive Anderson

Through The British Museum with the Bible

Brian Edwards
Clive Anderson

NEW   TRAVEL WITH JONATHAN EDWARDS

Born in the wilds of America, on the very edge of the British Empire, his books and thought revolutionized his world, and today he is recognized as the leading theologian of the eighteenth century. A fascinating Journey with Jonathan Edwards.
By **Michael Haykin** with Ron Baines.

Jonathan **Edwards**
A God-centered life, an enduring legacy

Michael Haykin with Ron Baines

Above: *Bayards Cove Dartmouth (UK), where* Mayflower *and* Speedwell *put in for repairs*

Acknowledgments

I am grateful to the following people for their invaluable help and assistance in preparing this book. Firstly my wife, for her willingness to spend our 30th wedding anniversary holiday wandering round graveyards!

I am also grateful to those who have made their photographs available for use in this book – particularly 'Daderot' and 'Swampyank' whose work on Wikipedia Commons filled several gaps in our photography. Thanks too to Ian and Jill Maxted for their kind permission to use several photographs of the Dutch city of Leiden.

Page 15 Boston Guildhall by Charistine Hasman
Page 29 Section of merchant-ship by User Mupshot on Wikipedia Commons
Page 35 First Encounter Beach plaque by Inacents (www.inacents.com)
Page 50 Forefather's monument, Plymouth by T S Custadio
Page 57 St Botolph's, by Bardofl
Page 64 Map of Pioneer Village by George Courage Creative
Page 72 Cuckoos Farm by Peterkirk
Page 79 Settlement of Plymouth colony (Map) by Hoodinski
Page 98 Rebecca Nurse Homestead by Wilijay
Page 109 Kings Chapel, Boston by Chensiyuan
Page 113 Boston Massacre Marker by Ingfbruno

Photographs of Mayflower II, the Wampanoag Village and Plimoth Plantation are the author's own images but we acknowledge the entitlement of Plimoth Plantation to be credited for their use.

Every effort has been made to correctly establish copyright owners. If we have inadvertently used a photograph without the correct attribution, we will be pleased to correct this in subsequent editions.